The Loneliness of Leadership

Danny Jones

ASSOCIATE EDITOR: HANNAH BAISLEY
COVER PHOTO:DANNY JONES

ISBN: 979-8-9885037-1-2

COVER DESIGN: ALAN ESPARZA
PUBLICATION DATA:

THE LONELINESS OF LEADERSHIP / DANNY JONES.

INCLUDES BIBLIOGRAPHICAL REFERENCES.
FOR PERMISSION REQUESTS, WRITE TO THE
PUBLISHER AT:

P.O. BOX 897
AIEA, HI 96782
INFO@IHICOACHING.COM
VISIT OUR WEBSITE AT:
HTTPS://WWW.IHICOACHING.COM/

DEDICATION

This book is dedicated to the leaders who have made the difficult sacrifices that come with great leadership. You may feel lonely and isolated, but you are definitely not alone.

SPECIAL THANKS
To all who have supported me and IHI Coaching throughout the years. Thank you to all of my models Alan, Brysen, Cammy, Christa, Cullen, Dominic, Elida, Kathryn, Kim, Mikael, Hannah, Shannon, Rylee, Yvette

CONTENTS

PREFACE

Leadership can be so very lonely. The fact of the matter is, in healthy leadership, the buck stops with you. You are responsible for your team and a failure of your team is your responsibility. The consequences of your decisions end up on your desk both positive and negative, and that can leave you very alone as you contemplate the variables.

There are also emotional issues that can wear you down that depending on your role, you can't just discuss with some random person or often times anyone on your team. To be clear, this is a Leadership book. There will be ideas and stories that come from my work as an executive coach as well as a Christian pastor, the concepts discussed here are universally best practices.

Throughout the book, you will hear stories of leaders I have sat under in churches as well as businesses. Whereas the guidance and comfort I receive as a leader are from what I call my Life Team, it ultimately comes from God. This book is not meant to preach to you, there will be no condemning or scolding but rather, just hopefully a reminder that you don't ever have to be completely alone as a leader.

I consider myself an executive coach and consultant who happens to write so, I am more interested in content than I am in having a literary masterpiece.

Before you waste your time on this book, I am going to suggest things that are often difficult or uncomfortable. Some things some of you may think are ridiculous or stupid, my question that I want you to ask yourself before even buying this book is, how badly do you want to break free from feeling lonely? How long do you want to last? Are you willing to do whatever it takes to make sure that this isolation is broken and doesn't lead you down a path that will be destructive for your life?

We are going to discuss many concepts of leadership in general as well as some of the pitfalls that a leader experiences. Also, I will share the tools I use with my clients to help them cope with that seclusion that leaders often feel. If you don't feel the things that we will discuss in this book, that's wonderful! I would encourage you to check in with the other leaders around you and see how they are doing and share the knowledge and tips you have with them as well.

As you read, you will come across a list of just some of the responsibilities and tasks that leaders undertake. There are specific reasons for this approach. Firstly, for individuals who aspire to become leaders, it is crucial to gain a full understanding of the multitude of challenges and responsibilities that leaders face on a daily basis. By exploring these aspects, readers who are not yet in leadership roles can develop a clearer perspective of the complexities of leadership and not hope after something that they are unprepared for.

For those already in leadership positions, some of the descriptions may resonate strongly with their own experiences, reaffirming that the demands they encounter are indeed part of their daily work. This recognition serves as a reminder that the weight of responsibility they carry is significant and should be acknowledged and appreciated.

I saw a television show many years ago that featured individuals with morbid obesity, the type who weighed in excess of 500 lbs. In the show, a health expert would display all the food consumed by one of the individuals in a single day on a table. The purpose was to shock them with the realization of the sheer quantity they were consuming. It often equated to what an entire family would consume in a week. Similarly, in this book, I aim to present leaders with a comprehensive view of all the challenges they face constantly. By highlighting the multitude of responsibilities, I hope to foster self-compassion and understanding among leaders. Sometimes, leaders may be so accustomed to dealing with these challenges that they fail to recognize the toll it takes on their well-being, leading to struggles and burnout.

By showcasing the breadth and depth of leadership responsibilities, I intend to provide leaders with a fresh perspective on their own experiences. It is my hope that this understanding will lead to greater self-compassion, enabling leaders to navigate their roles with grace and resilience. It is my belief that the beginning of breaking out of loneliness is being able to acknowledge what you are going through and to give yourself an allowance for mistakes and the magnitude of what you are dealing with.

This book is intended for people at all levels of leadership as well as those considering taking on a role in leadership. As such, some concepts are very deep while others may be ideas you have known for a long time.

Another caveat: this book will have quite a variety of paradoxes; Make sure you keep your dreams quiet so people don't stomp on them and discourage you/make sure you share your dreams with those you trust so you can be open and encouraged along the way. One important role of a leader is to find a way to navigate these lines that seem oppositional.

INTRODUCTION

I was at a healing conference years ago where the pastor was well known for being the guy who prayed for people and they got healed, (If you don't believe in this stuff don't worry about it, the concept is generally applicable and I will explain how after.) He shared a story about how there was a woman who brought her 5-year-old daughter to him who was truly at the end of her rope. Whatever the medical issue she had, the doctors said there was nothing left to do. This man looked at this adorable child and with all the faith in the world he prayed for her, completely sure that she was going to be healed. Unfortunately, he got word a few weeks later that the little girl passed away.

This pastor was absolutely distraught. He had seen many people healed in his life that he prayed for so, why not this innocent child? He also struggled with the fact that he felt like there was no one he could discuss it with. He was angry with God and had moments of doubt, but how was a pastor supposed to discuss these feelings with his staff? He felt couldn't because he worried what type of example that would have set for them. It took several years before he felt like it was okay for him to share this experience with others.

You don't have to believe in God to understand that when you have one job. Just one, and for whatever reason you fail or feel like you have failed, it can be devastating. You are the leader of your company and you hear about this new thing that you want to implement so, with all excitement you put your stamp on this new initiative. Then the initiative fails, and the emotions that you feel can be overwhelming. Often times we will start to get angry and try to put the blame on people because we don't want to face the emotions that are there.

If you are a publicly traded company, your failure can be mitigated but, if you go out and share too much of how you feel and the surrounding fears or emotions, you may end up damaging shareholder confidence causing a potentially catastrophic fallout. It's no wonder leaders often have to hide how they are feeling and doing. The problem that we will discuss in this book is that keeping all of these things to yourself will either manifest in poor leadership, ie... lashing out at subordinates or your family, or others. Or it may end with you shortening your life or causing burnout and losing your position.

One of the behaviors that we will be discussing is people's intention and how it communicates. For example, if you have contempt for someone, it will leak out through your words, body language, and tone, even if your actions seem to be neutral. Similarly, frustration and unrealistic expectations can show through our non-verbal communication. Throughout this book, we will reference this concept to help explain some of the ways the pressure is placed on leaders as well as how leaders can help to create a more communal environment.

A HISTORY OF LEADERSHIP

The corporate world and the military may seem like disparate domains, yet the roots of corporate leadership structure can be traced back to the military. In ancient civilizations like the Roman Empire, ancient China, and medieval Europe, military organizations played a crucial role in maintaining order, expanding territories, and protecting their respective realms. These civilizations employed hierarchical structures that facilitated efficient command and control. In the Roman Empire, the military was organized into legions, each led by a commander known as a Legatus. The legions were further divided into cohorts, centuries, and maniples, each with its own hierarchy of officers. This hierarchical system ensured clear lines of authority, with commanders at various levels responsible for the discipline, training, and strategic decisions of their units.

Similarly, in ancient China, military organizations were structured around the concept of the "Three Camps and Nine Divisions." The military hierarchy consisted of a general at the top, followed by various ranks of officers and soldiers. The hierarchical structure allowed for effective coordination and unified command, with each division responsible for a specific role, such as infantry, cavalry, or archers. The strict adherence to hierarchy ensured discipline, loyalty, and obedience among the troops, crucial for maintaining order and effectiveness in battles.

In medieval Europe, the feudal system shaped military organizations. Knights served as the primary warriors and commanders, pledging loyalty and military service to their lords. The hierarchical structure was based on the notion of vassalage, where knights owed allegiance to higher-ranking nobles in exchange for land or protection. This system created a clear chain of command, with lords having authority over their vassals, who, in turn, commanded their contingent of troops. The hierarchical structure enabled feudal lords to mobilize and deploy forces efficiently, reinforcing their power and maintaining social order within their territories.

These early military organizations and their hierarchical structures in ancient civilizations laid the foundation for future military practices and influenced the development of organizational structures in other domains, including the corporate world. The emphasis on hierarchy, discipline, and command allowed for effective coordination, decision-making, and control in the face of various challenges encountered by these ancient civilizations.

The command-and-control model, characterized by the chain of command and a strong emphasis on discipline and obedience, is a hierarchical leadership structure commonly associated with military organizations. In this model, authority flows from the top down, with clear lines of communication and decision-making. The chain of command establishes a formal structure in which each individual reports to a superior, who, in turn, reports to their superior, creating a vertical hierarchy. Discipline and obedience are paramount, as military operations require strict adherence to orders and protocols. This model emphasizes the need for a well-defined hierarchy, where leaders possess authority and subordinates are expected to follow instructions promptly and without question. The command-and-control model aims to ensure effective coordination, coordination, and unity of effort in achieving military objectives, relying on the disciplined execution of orders within the established chain of command.

The Industrial Revolution, spanning from the 18th to the 19th century, marked a significant shift in the way goods were produced. With the advent of new technologies, such as steam power and mechanized systems, traditional craftsmanship gave way to large-scale industrial operations. This transformational shift had a drastic impact on the emergence of modern business organizational structure. The need for increased production efficiency and economies of scale drove the consolidation of smaller, decentralized workshops into larger factories. Centralized control became crucial in managing these vast industrial operations, where coordination and oversight were necessary to ensure smooth operations, optimal resource allocation, and quality control. Business leaders recognized the advantages of centralized decision-making and coordination to achieve productivity gains and compete in the rapidly evolving market landscape.

Centralized control and coordination were vital in large-scale industrial operations during the Industrial Revolution. The scale of production and the complexity of industrial processes demanded a centralized authority to oversee various functions, including procurement, production planning, resource allocation, and distribution. Centralized control allowed for better coordination among different departments and facilitated the standardization of production processes. It ensured that operations ran smoothly and efficiently, minimizing wastage and maximizing output. Additionally, centralized control provided a mechanism for enforcing discipline and ensuring adherence to established rules and procedures. With a clear chain of command and authority, decisions could be made swiftly and implemented across the organization, streamlining operations and improving overall productivity.

In scripture, Moses was placed over a leadership contingent of those leading "Thousands, Hundreds, Fifty's and Tens." This is not far off from the leadership model used in military settings only the Jewish people of the time lived under a theocracy, the final authority was God. It is often hailed as being a great leader when we can show how hard we work, how many hours we are putting in etc. That said, in Exodus 18, Jethro: Moses' father comes to him and says, you can't do this, it's not good. We need someone in our life who will remind us that we are in fact human, and only capable of what we are capable of.

Furthermore, I would like to propose an alternative leadership style that has people on a slightly more even field. I don't subscribe to the leadership modality where everyone is completely equal because it resembles anarchy in my mind. However, I am generally not going recommend anyone change their core leadership structure but, I am saying that if you implement the things in this book, you may end up having things look very different. The difference is something that you need to be prepared to handle. If you are used to just giving commands and people moving without question and are not open to an alternative, many of these changes won't work out.

During the First and Second World Wars, we were more or less sending children off to war. When those who survived came home, their only professional experience was war. They also didn't have much in the way of post-secondary education. They did, however, know how to follow orders. So many of the corporations that were built in that time were soldiers who were looking to their former commanders who had gone into the private sector or someone to tell them what to do.

People who haven't had military procedures and thinking drilled into them from a young age and then forged in combat, struggle with this methodology. For combat, it's a system that works and is necessary. However, in the non-military world, this is damning for creativity, health, and longevity. To be clear, in the military, this pecking order where you are not allowed to question authority outside of very specific scenarios, is for your health and longevity. But if no one is shooting at you, then this is not helpful or conducive to growth.

Throughout this book, there will be a lot of talk about being open to new ideas from your employees or those beneath you in the organizational structure so buckle in and get ready. It may be a wild journey for some of you.

THE DANGERS OF LONELINESS

Lions always attack the slowest zebra or the animal that is alone. If you believe in the concept of sin and temptation, the Bible says that the lion is waiting to pounce. If you don't, know this, there are people waiting to take your job, to put your business out because you are the competition. When you are alone that is when it is the easiest to attack.

A few years ago a client shared a story with me about their previous mentor. The mentor told my client I will call Shawn, what to do, and how to do his job well. But he never taught Shawn how to open up with his feelings, and if he was having difficulties with his work. Shawn later learned that it was because his mentor didn't have an idea of how to do so himself. This became painfully apparent when his mentor began to behave erratically and his performance began to dissipate. He went from being the top guy in the company to missing work, getting angry, and blowing up at people around him. One day he was escorted out of the building in handcuffs. Sadly, the mentor had turned to drugs and alcohol. One day an employee found a large amount of drugs sitting on his desk under a file.

After the mentor dealt with his legal trouble and went to a mandated treatment program he shared with Shawn that he didn't know how to share about the struggles of the pressure of the job. He didn't know how to ask for help and he truly thought that he would be able to do it all on his own. He told Shawn that it was a dangerous trap to fall into and he recommended doing whatever it takes to not fall himself. Thankfully Shawn knew a former client of mine and decided to call me. I was able to be his confidential listener and help him process his stresses. As he became accustomed to sharing he was able to be open with coworkers as well.

Loneliness and isolation can have significant detrimental effects on leaders, permeating every aspect of their lives and their ability to lead effectively. When leaders find themselves isolated and cut off from meaningful connections and support, they often experience a sense of disconnection and detachment. This loneliness can lead to decreased motivation, diminished creativity, and a lack of inspiration. It can erode their confidence, self-esteem, and overall well-being, causing stress, anxiety, and even depression. Moreover, the absence of a strong support system and the feeling of being alone in decision-making can amplify the pressure and weight of leadership responsibilities. Loneliness can hinder leaders' ability to communicate effectively, collaborate with others, and build trusting relationships, ultimately impacting team dynamics and organizational performance. Recognizing the detrimental impact of isolation, leaders must proactively address this issue, seeking connection, support, and opportunities for growth to unlock their full potential and foster a thriving leadership journey.

You may be reading some of these things and thinking, "Well, yeah that's why I bought this book." Others may not have even realized where the lack of motivation came from. Wherever you are, I aim to help you find your way out of the hole that you may be in.

The potential negative consequences of loneliness and isolation for both individuals and organizations are profound. When leaders experience isolation, it can lead to a range of negative outcomes that reverberate throughout the entire organization. On an individual level, prolonged isolation can significantly impact mental health, leading to increased levels of stress, anxiety, and even depression. The absence of meaningful connections and support systems deprives leaders of the emotional nourishment and perspective needed to navigate the challenges of leadership effectively.

Furthermore, isolation can contribute to burnout, as leaders bear the weight of their responsibilities without the necessary outlets for rejuvenation and support. The constant pressure and lack of connection can drain their energy, hinder their ability to cope with stress, and ultimately compromise their well-being. This, in turn, can lead to decreased productivity, reduced engagement, and increased turnover rates within the organization.

Isolation also has a direct impact on decision-making. When leaders are cut off from diverse perspectives and input, they may become prone to biased thinking, limited insights, and tunnel vision. Without the benefit of collaboration and healthy dialogue, decisions may be made in isolation and lack the necessary considerations for long-term success. This can have detrimental effects on the organization, leading to poor strategic choices, missed opportunities, and diminished innovation.

Recognizing the profound connection between isolation and mental health, burnout, and decision-making, it is crucial for leaders and organizations to prioritize developing an inclusive and supportive environment. Encouraging open communication, establishing networks of support, and promoting a culture that values collaboration and well-being are essential steps to mitigate the negative consequences of isolation and create an environment where individuals and organizations can thrive.

Within the realm of leadership, the allure of maintaining the status quo and avoiding discomfort can be a powerful force that keeps leaders trapped in isolation. It is human nature to seek stability and familiarity, and the prospect of stepping outside of one's comfort zone can be daunting. The fear of the unknown, the potential for failure, and the discomfort of confronting one's vulnerabilities can all contribute to a tendency toward the familiar, even if it means living in isolation.

There are several reasons why leaders may choose to live with isolation rather than confront it. Firstly, there may be a misguided belief that isolation is synonymous with strength and independence. Leaders may perceive the need for connection and support as a sign of weakness, fearing that reaching out for help will undermine their authority or competence. This misconception perpetuates a cycle of isolation, preventing leaders from recognizing the benefits of collaboration and shared experiences.

Almost every DC and Marvel superhero movie and tv show model that being the hero means doing it alone. However, even the writers show that as powerful as all these heroes are, they all need to team up once in a while, thus, the Avengers and Justice League exist. It is ingrained in so many people to think that my strength is modeled in the fact that, "I did this alone." But the truth is, if you did that on your own, there are unimaginable things you could have accomplished if you included a team with you.

Moreover, confronting isolation requires introspection and self-awareness, which can be challenging and uncomfortable. It necessitates acknowledging and addressing one's own limitations, insecurities, and blind spots. This level of vulnerability can be intimidating, leading leaders to opt for the familiar discomfort of isolation rather than embarking on the potentially transformative journey of self-discovery and growth.

However, accepting isolation as the norm carries significant risks. By isolating themselves, leaders deprive themselves of valuable perspectives, feedback, and support that can enhance their decision-making and overall effectiveness. They miss out on the opportunity to foster meaningful connections, build strong relationships, and create a culture of trust within their organization. Furthermore, living in isolation can lead to a sense of detachment and disengagement, both personally and professionally, resulting in diminished motivation, creativity, and productivity.

To break free from the allure of maintaining the status quo and avoiding discomfort, leaders must recognize the potential risks of accepting isolation as the norm. They need to embrace the inherent value of connection, collaboration, and vulnerability. By acknowledging the benefits of stepping out of their comfort zones, leaders can cultivate a mindset of growth, resilience, and continuous learning. This shift in perspective opens the door to new possibilities, cultivates a sense of belonging, and ultimately enhances their effectiveness as leaders.

In leadership, it is crucial to encourage leaders to step outside their comfort zones and embrace growth. Growth occurs when we push ourselves beyond familiar boundaries, challenge our assumptions, and venture into uncharted territories. By embracing discomfort, leaders can unlock new levels of personal and professional development, leading to greater resilience, adaptability, and success.

Challenging oneself and seeking new experiences bring numerous benefits to leaders. Firstly, it broadens their perspective and enhances their ability to navigate complex and ever-changing landscapes. By exposing themselves to diverse ideas, cultures, and perspectives, leaders gain fresh insights and alternative approaches to problem-solving. This expanded mindset enables them to make more informed decisions, think creatively, and effectively respond to challenges.

Stepping outside the comfort zone creates personal growth and self-discovery. It helps leaders uncover hidden strengths, develop new skills, and build confidence in their abilities. By embracing discomfort, leaders demonstrate a willingness to learn and adapt, setting an example for their teams and fostering a culture of growth within the organization.

To support leaders in expanding their comfort zones and embracing discomfort, practical techniques can be employed. One effective approach is setting small, achievable goals that progressively stretch their boundaries. By taking incremental steps outside the comfort zone, leaders can gradually build confidence and resilience. Additionally, seeking feedback and learning from failure is essential in the growth process. Leaders should view setbacks as learning opportunities, extract valuable lessons, and apply them to future endeavors.

Another technique is actively seeking new experiences and challenges. This could involve attending conferences, workshops, or seminars, engaging in cross-functional collaborations, or taking on new responsibilities within the organization. By deliberately exposing themselves to unfamiliar situations, leaders can cultivate a sense of curiosity, adaptability, and openness to change.

Ultimately, by encouraging leaders to step outside their comfort zones, embrace growth, and seek new experiences, organizations can foster a culture of continuous improvement, innovation, and resilience. Leaders who are willing to confront discomfort and push their limits inspire their teams to do the same, creating an environment that nurtures creativity, collaboration, and high performance.

THE WEIGHT OF RESPONSIBILITY

Leadership comes with a significant weight of responsibility that can have a profound impact on leaders themselves. The burden of responsibility encompasses a range of factors, including the well-being and success of the team, the organization's performance, and the consequences of their decisions. Firstly, leaders are entrusted with the task of guiding and supporting their team members, ensuring their growth, development, and overall well-being. The weight of responsibility lies in their duty to create a conducive work environment, foster a culture of collaboration and engagement, and address any challenges or conflicts that arise within the team.

Secondly, leaders are responsible for the success and performance of the organization. They are expected to make strategic decisions, set goals, allocate resources, and drive progress toward achieving the organization's objectives. The weight of responsibility rests on their ability to navigate uncertainties, mitigate risks, and adapt to the changing business landscape. The outcomes of their decisions can have far-reaching implications for the organization, its stakeholders, and even the broader community.

Leaders bear the weight of responsibility for the impact of their decisions on individual lives. Their choices may result in changes to the organization's structure, policies, or even workforce. This responsibility extends to ensuring fairness in the decision-making processes, considering the potential consequences for employees, and striving to minimize any negative impacts. The weight of responsibility lies in the knowledge that their decisions can influence the livelihoods and careers of those they lead.

Leaders also shoulder the responsibility of being role models and exemplifying the values and ethics of the organization. They are expected to be transparent, ethical and make decisions with integrity at all times. The weight of responsibility lies in the need to maintain trust and credibility, both within the organization and among external stakeholders. Leaders understand that their behavior sets the tone for the entire organization, and they must make choices that align with the organization's values and promote its long-term sustainability.

The weight of responsibility that leaders carry can be immense and can manifest in various ways, including stress, pressure, and emotional strain. Recognizing and acknowledging this weight is crucial for leaders to proactively manage their well-being, seek support when needed, and develop coping mechanisms to handle the challenges they face. Effective leadership requires leaders to navigate this responsibility with grace, resilience, and a commitment to serving the best interests of their team, organization, and wider society.

Leadership experiences are often misunderstood by those who haven't held leadership positions. I have worked under leaders who were not particularly skilled in leadership but still faced the weight of their decisions. Years ago, I consulted for a leader who owned a construction company but lacked effective communication skills. This was just the beginning of the leadership challenges he combated. He struggled to delegate tasks and would frequently intervene and impose his own methods, hindering the growth and development of the leaders below him.

As a result, lower-level leaders never had the opportunity to learn how to lead effectively or fulfill the boss's expectations. Additionally, his tendency to override the work of other leaders undermined their efforts and disrupted established plans and schedules.

Although his behavior appeared as a lack of concern for his management team, private conversations with him revealed his underlying worry. He shared that his constant need to intervene and "fix" things stemmed from the fear that if those beneath him didn't perform their jobs adequately, the company would fail, leaving employees and their families living on the street without food. The paradox of leadership lies in the delicate balance between training and empowering those under your guidance, allowing them room to make mistakes, and implementing safeguards to protect both individuals and the organization.

Leadership entails the responsibility to nurture and develop the skills of those working under you while simultaneously creating an environment that safeguards against potential failures. It requires finding the right balance between trust and support, understanding that mistakes are a part of growth, and implementing measures that mitigate risks. Effective leadership involves training, mentoring, and providing opportunities for growth while acknowledging the inherent uncertainties and challenges of the leadership journey.

From what I've seen and experienced, leadership comes with its fair share of emotional struggles. You often find yourself facing dilemmas where there's no easy answer. You second-guess yourself, lose sleep over decisions, and worry about failing. It can sometimes feel like you are carrying the weight of the world on your shoulders.

On top of that, the choices you make as a leader can have a huge impact on people's lives. Whether it's restructuring the organization, making changes that affect job security, or dealing with team conflicts, you have to consider the well-being and livelihoods of your employees. You genuinely care about them, and that adds an extra layer of emotional burden to your already heavy load.

Sometimes, the pressure to appear strong and composed all the time can contribute to the feeling of isolation. As a leader, people expect you to have it all figured out. There can be a strong temptation to fake it no matter what. There is a place for projecting confidence and at times it's very necessary, however, there still must be time where you can share honestly and allow for the truth.

Recognizing the emotional toll that leadership takes is crucial. We need to create environments that encourage leaders to prioritize their well-being. It's important to give them the space and support to address their emotional needs, seek guidance, and connect with peers who understand what they're going through. By acknowledging the emotional challenges of leadership and promoting open dialogue, we can create a culture that supports and uplifts leaders, helping them navigate the ups and downs with a healthier mindset.

Leadership is often hailed as a position of power, influence, and success. We admire leaders for their ability to inspire others, make tough decisions, and drive organizations forward. Yet, beneath the surface of authority and admiration lies an aspect of leadership that is frequently overlooked: loneliness.

Leadership can be an isolating experience. When we envision leaders, we often picture them standing at the helm, confidently leading the way. However, behind closed doors, leaders face challenges that few can truly understand. They bear the weight of responsibility for the well-being of their team, the success of their organization, and the impact of their decisions. This burden can be overwhelming and emotionally draining.

The loneliness of leadership emerges from several sources. First and foremost is the burden of responsibility. Leaders are entrusted with making difficult choices that impact the lives and livelihoods of others. They must navigate complex problems, juggle competing priorities, and make decisions that are often fraught with uncertainty. In such moments, the weight of responsibility rests solely on their shoulders, and the fear of making mistakes can be paralyzing.

Leaders face what is known as the expectations gap. They are expected to exude strength, confidence, and unwavering resolve. This external perception often leads to the suppression of vulnerability, as leaders fear that showing their doubts or seeking support may undermine their authority or create uncertainty among their team. Consequently, leaders may find themselves isolated, unable to share their true thoughts and feelings, and lacking a safe space to express their vulnerabilities.

Another contributing factor to the loneliness of leadership is the paradox of power. While leaders may possess authority and control, they can feel disconnected from those they lead. The hierarchical nature of leadership often creates a barrier between leaders and their team members. They must maintain professional boundaries, which can hinder the formation of genuine connections. The loneliness arises from the inability to bridge this gap and create meaningful relationships that go beyond the confines of the professional sphere.

Decision-making, too, can be a solitary endeavor for leaders. They are expected to make tough choices, often in high-pressure situations, with limited time and information. The weight of these decisions can be overwhelming, and the process can feel incredibly lonely. Leaders may long for someone to share the burden, to provide guidance or validation, but ultimately, the responsibility falls squarely on their shoulders. This isolation in decision-making can contribute to the sense of loneliness that accompanies leadership.

The personal sacrifices leaders make can also contribute to their loneliness. They often dedicate significant time and energy to their roles, sometimes at the expense of their personal lives. Strained relationships, a lack of work-life balance, and the limited opportunity for self-care can further deepen the sense of isolation. As leaders pour themselves into their work, they may find fewer connections outside of it, exacerbating their loneliness.

Recognizing and addressing the loneliness of leadership is crucial for leaders' well-being and their ability to effectively lead. Leaders must seek support networks, both within and outside their organizations, where they can find understanding, guidance, and empathy. Embracing vulnerability and creating a culture of openness and trust within their teams can help alleviate the isolation. It is essential for leaders to prioritize self-care, establish boundaries, and engage in activities that nourish their personal lives.

By acknowledging and addressing the loneliness of leadership, we can foster environments that support leaders' emotional well-being and, in turn, enhance their capacity to lead with purpose and authenticity. Leadership need not be a lonely journey; with the right strategies and support, leaders can find solace, connection, and fulfillment in their roles.

THE SPACE BETWEEN:
EXPECTATIONS VS. REALITY

Leaders are often hailed as these infallible perfect people who are just monsters when they make a mistake. If they do something that offends or hurts someone then they must have done it intentionally because leaders know what they are doing and how they are doing it at all times. There is so often an expectation that is probably based on small snippets of every leader they have seen on TV or in their lives or stories, sewn together to create what they are thinking their boss should be like. It is not dissimilar to the vastly outside-of-reality view that people have before going into a relationship.

Leadership is often put on a pedestal, surrounded by sky-high expectations. We imagine leaders as these flawless, all-knowing superheroes who can tackle any challenge thrown their way. But the truth is, leaders are just human beings with their strengths and weaknesses. In this chapter, we're going to dive into the vast gap between what's expected of leaders and what they're capable of. We'll explore the challenges they face and the importance of embracing leadership as an ongoing learning journey. There are exceptional leaders, and as with all skills, there are people with more skill and greater capacity, but at the end of the day, they are human beings.

Nobody's perfect, and that includes leaders. Yet, society loves to paint this picture of leaders who never stumble, always have the right answers, and effortlessly steer their organizations toward success. Leaders have their limitations and struggles. They may excel in some areas but fall short in others. It's crucial to understand that leaders are not infallible or all-knowing. By recognizing their humanity and embracing their imperfections, we can let go of unrealistic expectations and allow leaders the space to learn, grow, and seek support when needed. As leaders, remembering this gives us more space for our shortcomings; as those who are following, this gives us a better understanding of who our leaders are and how we can support them.

This common distortion leads to problems for both the leader and those following. Leaders can tell when someone has unrealistic expectations. They can also usually tell when they have not met those expectations and there is dissension in the leader-subordinate relationship. This can weigh heavily on the leader. Yes, a great leader learns how to deal with the sense of regular disappointment and even learns tricks and tools to mitigate overly high expectations. However, leaders are just human beings with feelings. Unfortunately, many leaders I have worked with have learned to cope with those feelings by masking anger or repressing all emotions and becoming stoic.

A mentor of mine once said that offense is based on the gap between expectation and reality. His example was if he tells his wife that he will be home at 6:00 and gets there at 6:00 no problems. If he gets there at maybe 6:15 possibly she would be a little irritated but unless the exact time was vital not too big of a deal. However, if he arrived home 2 hours late, there is going to be problems. The gap between expectation and reality is where offense grows.

Similarly, when a subordinate has an expectation of when something will start, or what will happen; The further reality lands from the expectation, the greater the offense. Of course, all of us have felt offended by something at some point in our lives and it is so easy to feel disconnection or desire to cut someone off when that emotion comes in. This is problematic when someone is offended by their leader. There is a great amount of difficulty in being led by someone you don't want to have a relationship with.

Leadership isn't about having a crystal ball or a foolproof roadmap. It's about steering the ship through stormy seas and adapting to constant changes. Yet, the expectations of leaders often demand quick fixes, clear-cut solutions, and unwavering confidence. Reality doesn't always work that way. The business world is full of uncertainty and constant changes. Leaders must make tough decisions with incomplete information, face unexpected challenges, and grapple with complex problems. Embracing the reality that leaders are navigating uncharted territory can help us adjust our expectations and allow them the space to make well-informed decisions in the face of ambiguity.

Leadership is not a one-size-fits-all, set-it-and-forget-it kind of deal. It's a continuous journey of growth and development. Yet, many expectations overlook this fact. We can't expect leaders to have all the answers from day one or possess every skill in the book. It's unrealistic. Instead, we should encourage leaders to embrace a mindset of continuous learning, seek feedback, and invest in their personal and professional growth. By acknowledging the reality that leadership skills are honed over time and embracing a culture of learning, leaders can bridge the gap between expectations and reality. It's through this growth journey that leaders become more effective, adaptable, and capable of inspiring their teams.

To bridge the gap between expectations and reality, we need to create an environment that supports leaders. It's time to shift away from the superhero narrative and build a culture that values transparency, vulnerability, and open communication. Leaders should feel comfortable acknowledging their limitations, asking for help, and building a network of support. When organizations foster a collaborative atmosphere that encourages learning from failures and sharing knowledge, leaders can navigate their roles with greater self-awareness and resilience.

The pressure to be strong, and confident, and always have the answers weighs heavily on leaders' shoulders. In the eyes of their teams and organizations, leaders are expected to exude unwavering strength and confidence, even in the face of adversity. They are seen as the guiding lights, the ones who possess the solutions to every problem. This pressure often leads leaders to internalize the belief that they must never show vulnerability or admit to not having all the answers. They feel compelled to project an image of infallibility, fearing that any sign of weakness will erode trust and confidence in their leadership. As a result, leaders may suppress their doubts, fears, and uncertainties, which can take a toll on their mental and emotional well-being.

I am personally guilty of going after leaders in my younger years with very cavalier and hurtful words, because, "They can take it." I felt at that time that these leaders were so strong and perfect that the only way I could get through to them was if I hit them with the strongest swing I had. I had to have a lot of apology conversations where I was asking for forgiveness for scathing words I spoke out of my youthful impetuousness. The belief that leaders are impervious to all things around them is so wrong and can even be dangerous, as I learned that my behavior often hurt leaders in the scenarios above.

As I will say often in this book, the burden of leadership is one that comes from the choice to take the mantle of leadership. However, not only are there times people are thrust into leadership and rise to the occasion out of necessity and a sense of duty, but again, they are human. They do deserve some grace and understanding. The isolation that a leader feels, especially when they are treated poorly by someone who is supposed to be trusted, someone who is supposed to have their back can be harrowing.

One of the things that I do with my life in ministry is musical worship, I speak at leadership or worship conferences in different countries around the world. As I mentioned in the church world, sometimes the person who stands on stage for whatever reason may end up being revered as more than a "normal" person. There are so many problems with this; as a Christian, there is clear scripture about all people being equal in the eyes of God, and further, there is a story in the bible about a man who accepted the praise of the people calling him equal to or a god, and he died instantly. But more understandably, I become very uncomfortable not only because I strongly dislike the feeling of being treated as some sort of deity but I know that when people start to view me as something more than a flawed human, I know that at some point, I will undoubtedly disappoint them. This disappointment can lead to a small or even catastrophic fallout depending on the scenario.

A particular example, again from my early days in a leadership role, someone approached me after one such conference and asked if we could get a cup of coffee. Not paying close enough attention to their body language and words, I agreed. Once we went for coffee we were discussing different topics and then at some point, they asked me a question, and I responded, I had no idea. The look of shock was startling to me. Their look of stunned expressions became almost disgusted as their picture of my infinite knowledge was being shattered. I was no longer who they were expecting. This I believe is one of the roots of the statement. "Never meet your hero." We paint a picture of who they are but in real life, they probably could never live up to it.

I was genuinely shocked by this interaction. During my childhood and teenage years, as with many teenagers, I thought I knew everything. One lesson I learned very quickly when I became an adult was how little about how little I truly knew.

Unfortunately, when you look up to someone, it is easy to create your own beliefs about them and describe them to yourself however you see fit. I try to be very clear with people now, that I am not perfect nor do I know all things. I have long gotten over the ego where I need people to think I am smart. As a leader, I had to come to grips with the fact that I know what I know, and I constantly pursue more knowledge and experience.

I guess I shouldn't have been shocked though, I used to carry the same belief about other leaders. I published a Christian devotional that had a chapter called "Finishing Strong." I have begun working on an entire book on the topic. When I was in my early 20s, I was a new Christian and trying to find leaders whose example I could follow because I was feeling like such a lost fool trying to become a man. I found some men online who were well-known leaders, I found some locally as well. I began to create a picture of who they were, and what their personal life was like, and through that, I had a concrete idea of how perfect their lives were. I was completely wrong. The number of these people who ended up having severe moral failures is so very vast. The problem, I had created a fantasy world where they were perfect and so when they failed I was devastated. Unfortunately, this type of thinking is not uncommon. People so quickly decide what a person is like without their input.

This is the significance of making sure that you are very clear about who you are and your intentions. Also be clear about your shortcomings, especially with yourself. Shouldering all the weight of responsibility without getting help when you need it is like bench pressing more than you are capable of alone in the gym. It is going to cause damage sooner or later. To be clear, I am for you pushing your limits, which can mean that you one day will lift more weight than you can handle. The humility to be able to ask for help is of great consequence but so is having someone there to hear you when you ask.

Years ago someone told me something that I have adopted as a belief myself. People are immensely confused about what the word entrepreneur means. An entrepreneur is not someone who just knows everything and can do anything. I hear people say, "Oh well, I am just an entrepreneur." When they are simply a small business owner. I truly believe that an entrepreneur is someone who is keenly aware of their strengths and weaknesses. They can define their needs and find people that can fill them creating a very effective team. A very simplistic example is as a small business owner will do all aspects of owning a company and not necessarily get very far or big because I can't let go of the reins in certain areas for whatever reason. As an entrepreneur knows, I can easily get distracted, I don't love cracking the whip on people and I hate accounting because I get lost in the numbers when I have to look at them for too long. It's time we began to open up to the idea that we don't have to do all things at all times. I still struggle with letting go of things at times, because I know that I can probably do it better. Here's the rub… If I never let go and have other people try, I will always probably be better and we will never get anywhere. However, if I offer up the opportunity for others to try, and yes, fail, It allows them to learn how to do that thing well and hopefully much better than I can.

If you have ever bought a tool that had multiple uses, most commonly, it is not going to do any one thing exceptionally well. Take the Army knives by Victorinox, they are exceptionally useful. The knives are very sharp and decently strong. The scissors will cut through things, the tweezers will pull small things out, the can opener will open cans, etc. However, I guarantee if you race someone with an electric can opener or a high-quality handheld can opener, they will overtake the Swiss-made knife. The same would go with the scissors or tweezer. Also if you need to cut a roast, they make a full-sized knife but the little multitool won't do it nearly as well. When you take apart that multitool and have each one function doing only its job you can get much higher quality and more effective work. Understandably this isn't always possible, sometimes you have to perform multiple jobs and that's okay. The goal should always be trying to get to a place where everyone has their job and they do it really well.

I believe the people in my life are aware of my limitations and where I excel. I try to create a culture where it's acceptable and even encouraged that people are transparent about these things. I also work very hard to break any delusion that I have all the answers. When I first started to move this way it was out of sheer frustration. I was so tired of people getting upset with me for not knowing about something they thought I should. I am not sure how long it would have taken for me to make that move if not for that frustration as motivation. I was very nervous that I would lose the respect of those I needed to lead. The opposite was true.

I was on a worship team at a church nearly 20 years ago. I was young but thought I was important and knew what I was doing. Not only was this not accurate but the level of that inaccuracy was thrust into my face one day. The team was broken into three parts, the vocal leaders, the band, and the choir. On this fateful day, the choir director says that she is having an inappropriate relationship with the leader of the band who was married to the leader of the vocals. It was like a giant hurricane with tornados in it that swept through on the day the ministry met together.

I went from thinking, "Oh yeah, if I had the chance, I could lead this team with no problem." To, "Who in the world was I kidding." The moment the entire team; A choir of eleven people, a vocal team of four leaders, and a band of five people were now handed over to me I was terrified inside. This was not the first moment of leadership for me but it was definitely the first time it was thrown at me with zero warning. Just like lifting the bar off the rack and seeing that I am not strong enough to bench press it back up, I decided that I would be honest with the team and where I felt my abilities were at that time.

I held a meeting with the team and said that our pastor would address the reason, but for the time being, all the other three leaders were going to be taking some time off and they were now having to report to me. I told them point blank, "I do not feel prepared for this in any way, I don't have the capacity to lead three teams of twenty people. I need all of you to start paddling this canoe with me." No one questioned me as a leader or tried to usurp what I was doing in any way. In fact, they helped me so much that they transformed everything regarding how I lead. They would regularly ask if I needed help with things, and they would offer to sing songs without an attitude if I declined their request. They truly came together and bought into the fact that I needed everyone to take ownership of their part on the team.

The craziest thing is that some of the most proficient worship leaders I know to this day were on that team with me and stepped up to the plate at that time. Part of bridging the gap between leadership reality and expectations is to bring them on the journey. Now this example is fairly specific, but if you bring on leaders to help you and to walk with you, especially in your areas of weakness it can have an incredible result. Disclaimer: you need to trust them from experience as well as vulnerability-based trust. In a later chapter, I will explain the difference and talk about one of the great minds that I learned about this concept.

THE POWER PARADOX

Being a leader comes with a level of inherent power. If there is no power then you probably aren't a leader. Now the paradox is that your character will determine what happens when you begin to realize and exert that power. Take this dark example: Art is created with your hands, music is written or often played with your hands, as are literary masterpieces or probably almost anything that you can think of. However, hands are also one of the top 3-5 most common murder weapons in the United States depending on which year and statistic you are looking at. Power isn't intrinsically bad or evil, it's just a tool. Again, who we are before, and while we are leaders will affect how we treat the power we are given. My father used to say, money doesn't make you evil, money makes you more of who you already were. If you were secretly evil and wanted to build a ray gun to take over the world then you might try that when you have money to do so. If you were always a generous and caring person, then when you have greater finances, you will be on a larger scale. Power is the same. It simply amplifies who you are. This is why there is great significance that you learn about the character of the person before you place them in a leadership role.

Power in leadership is the ability to influence others and drive change within an organization or a team. It is the capacity to make decisions, allocate resources, and shape the direction of a group. Power is significant in leadership as it enables leaders to mobilize individuals towards a common goal, inspire commitment, and facilitate effective decision-making. It provides leaders with the authority and leverage needed to navigate challenges, resolve conflicts, and drive organizational success.

The paradoxical nature of power in leadership stems from its dual effects and challenges. On one hand, power can elevate leaders, granting them authority, influence, and the ability to make impactful decisions. It can instill confidence and inspire others to follow. However, on the other hand, power can be seductive, leading to ego-driven behavior, detachment from the needs of others, and the potential for corruption. The impact of this paradox is that leaders must navigate the fine line between using power responsibly and succumbing to its pitfalls. It requires self-awareness, humility, and a commitment to ethical leadership to ensure that power is wielded in a way that benefits both the organization and the individuals within it.

You can have the best ideas in the world that will be absolutely successful but if you have no influence or power, they will likely never get implemented- at least not until someone with power decides they like the idea. At which point it may or may not still be "your idea." That is to say, nothing changes without power and influence. However, there is an old adage credited to Lord Acton that says, "Absolute power corrupts absolutely." I don't know if I believe that, but I will say that the greater the level of power, the greater and stronger the character of the person must be.

It's a strange feeling having power for the first time, I coached the founder of a successful startup. It was fascinating to hear his story as he shared, there was this monster that started to come out from within the more successful that he became. He grew up poor, as a result, he didn't have much and so he was bullied a lot when he was young. So when he finally had the power of finances he found himself treating people around him, especially people in the service or trades very poorly. One day he snapped at a hotel concierge and was absolutely nasty to them. A friend who had been with him since the beginning pulled him aside and pointed out that he would never have let someone talk to his family like that before he was successful and most of his family worked in "menial" jobs. That's when he called me.

There is a proverb in the bible
> "Under three things the earth trembles,
> under four it cannot bear up:
> a servant who becomes king,

There is a very famous story in the bible that you have probably heard of, especially if you've seen the movie The Prince of Egypt. It is the story of Moses. Moses was a Jewish-born male who was saved from the annihilation Pharoah had set fourth of all young Jewish boys at that time. He was put in a basket in the river and found by the daughter of Pharoah. She took him in and raised him in the palace as her own. When the time came, Moses was called by God to lead all of the children of Israel out of Egypt's captivity.

This story is fascinating to me. From a psychological perspective, there is a direct relationship between the proverb and the story of Moses. I believe that the proverb says that the earth cannot handle a servant becoming a king because there is a powerful grasp that poverty has on the mind of the person raised in it. This is often why the children of wealthy families continue to be wealthy and conversely, those born into poverty struggle with developing and even more than that, sustaining wealth. Yes, the parents can help the children financially but far more importantly, the parent teaches the child how to make, keep, and handle money. Another example is when a person who has no experience with large amounts of money wins the lottery and ends up in worse shape within a few years. They are often not raised with the character or knowledge of how to handle that much money that fast.

In the story about Moses, he was raised as a king. He was taught leadership principles of the time and told that he was not a slave and that he was one of the highest-level leaders in all of the kingdom. This I believe was the plan that God had in order to be able to have a leader capable of leading millions of people through a desert. Is it impossible to teach this type of character? No, but it is far more difficult than teaching someone a set of skills.

Character is so important to contain the power that comes from being a leader. It is also how a person is able to maintain healthy relationships the higher they are elevated. If you compare power to magnetic polarities, a magnet either attracts or repels. The greater the power it has, the more it attracts or repels.

If a person had problems with authority because perhaps they were abused in some way by a person who was a leader when they were growing up, or at a previous job, the more powerful a person becomes, the more they will struggle with being an effective leader themselves. I have coached people who have a completely inexplicable problem with their boss. They will talk about how their boss is kind to them but no matter what happens when the boss comes around they are filled with anxiety.

I had a client who almost passed out once because her anxiety built and built each time her boss came around. It was such an interesting scenario because my client did her job very well, and received many awards for her performance. Her boss was always kind to her because she thought she was a great employee. As her coach, I found her to be a very nice person. However, she would just lose herself when the boss came around. After her dizzy spell, she decided to call me. After a few coaching sessions, she started to share about her mother and some issues she had with her that started in childhood and haven't gotten much better. I ended up referring her to a counselor who was able to help her manage the issues she had from her childhood, (I am a coach not a mental health professional – my purview is very specific.) After a few months, she was able to express to me what was going on. Her mother was extremely controlling and had her hand in everything my client did growing up and even to this day. Since her boss was highly respected and wielded a lot of power, she felt extremely triggered by her. She said that she was unable to function because her career was the one place where she was in control of her life.

It wasn't anything the leader had done that was isolating the leader. This is one of the paradoxes of the power that leaders possess. The power the leader had was actually able to help her if she had opened up, the leader could have demonstrated what healthy treatment could have looked like.

As a leader, it can be very difficult but so helpful to bridge the gap in the relationship with the subordinate. One of the many hurdles that a leader can encounter is that since so many people have their preconceptions of what a leader is and should be, some feel it's weird or inappropriate for the leader to be on the same level as the employee. Think about a time when there was a backyard BBQ where it was mostly employees but then the boss shows up. Everyone gets very strange in their behavior and attitude. Now this isn't always the case, and it can often become a very wonderful thing as everyone begins to open up and get used to the idea, but it often starts feeling a little strange.

As a leader, you need to take the leap and look for the balance between being the boss and being a part of the team. This may take a lot of adjustments including possibly adjusting the members of your team. As a leader, you need a team who is able to joke around and have fun at the same time respect each other and get the job done. A pastor of mine is fantastic at this skill. I was with him in a healing ministry where we were in a small group. One moment, we were all laughing and having a great time, and then next he was asking an extremely difficult question to one of the attendees. The grace at which he switched from having fun to asking someone about the abuse they received as a child was brilliant. It was so smooth that no one even reacted to the transition. This is an art that he has worked many years to perfect and it is such a powerful to have in your toolbelt.

When you work on becoming a leader that is relatable, you are unfortunately faced with all of those misconceptions that other leaders have taught your team. For example, the main one that I have experienced is when a leader becomes authentic, subordinates freak out because they have never experienced that type of honesty and their perception of perfection is broken. That can be difficult for people to understand and get used to. As they struggle through that it can open doors to a very powerful relationship. But just like almost every suggestion for transformation in this book, there will be strong growing pains. Also, the pendulum may swing a little far to one side or the other and back and forth until it lands in a comfortable place.

Leaders must grasp the weight of responsibility that accompanies their power. It entails recognizing that their decisions and actions have far-reaching consequences, impacting the lives and well-being of those they lead. Understanding this responsibility means acknowledging that leadership is not solely about personal gain, but rather about serving the collective interests of the organization and its members. Leaders should embrace the accountability that comes with their power and make decisions that prioritize the long-term success and welfare of their team. Having authenticity and a relationship where people know that you are human and that you may make mistakes is the easiest way to mitigate the fallout from the mistakes we will all inevitably make.

Finding an appropriate boundary line can be extremely difficult at times. On one hand, no one should be getting up in the middle of the night to fix a problem. When you are done, you should be done. That said, I realize that some of you may have roles where someone could literally die if you don't get up and attend to the issue. While others may lose millions of dollars or countless jobs.

I can't tell you where to draw the line, but I will say if the problem will be the same in the morning then you should probably let it be. Also, if the problem keeps happening or if there are different problems that seem to never go away then maybe it's time to evaluate things and decide if there is a change that needs to be made in your leadership style or even your team.

With setting these boundaries you also need to make sure that you are continuing to be fair in what you are doing and how you are behaving. A good example is once a good friend who needed a ringer as he said at the new company he had been hired as VP at. He asked me if I could come in and help him out with the work that he was acquiring. Although he and his wife and I have been close for over 10 years he still wanted to make sure there was some professional insulation. He put me under another leader who now worked for him. There is nothing wrong with hiring someone you know, especially if you are hiring them because of their skill. However, you definitely need to consider long and hard if they are just your friend and you have no professional context for them. If you do end up hiring someone you know, make sure that you do what you need to, to make sure that your professionalism is never called into question.

Again one of the issues that you are going to face is most of this book will talk about creating healthy boundaries all the while being honest and vulnerable when it's appropriate to develop a genuine connection between you the leader and those you serve. Maintaining an understanding of the fact that you are going to get it wrong and make mistakes is going to vastly benefit you over the long term. While you prepare yourself to be wrong and make mistakes, it will take some of the fear and discomfort out of being open with those around you.

One of the more underutilized tools that we can develop is emotional intelligence. It has gained more traction and is more integrated into many companies now than before. Emotional intelligence can often feel like a touchy-feely kumbaya circle but truly it's not. There is far more to it than that. Emotional intelligence on the surface is simply knowing yourself and understanding your emotions. Taking it further it's also about understanding other people's emotions and how they affect their work, their relationships, and their day-to-day lives.

I will probably end up saying this multiple times in the book but I do believe that overall as a society we have gotten overly soft. Everyone is offended about something or another and they need you to know that they are. This needs to stop. On the other hand, the world that I grew up in was professionally run by tyrants who didn't care about your feelings or what you wanted to do with your life. You were viewed as just part of the machine and nothing more. This was stifling creativity and was the largest contributor to my burning out. If we find a way to meet in the middle there would be so much productivity.

I had a client once who was the boss of a medium-sized advertising firm. He had the potential to be great. He truly cared about others and was really good at what he did. He was, however, totally and completely emotionally inept. His workload would begin to pile up on him and he would begin to systematically remove his worker's faces until they all wanted to quit. Not just because they didn't like his treatment, but also because by the time he was done with them, they all felt like they were terrible at their jobs and were useless. They were not. They were great employees, the boss told me himself. He was absolutely clueless about how his emotions would get the best of him and he would become a raving lunatic. There was a moment when one of his best employees finally snapped in his office after one of his many tirades. His employee with great performance records always had a decent attitude, great attendance lost it. The boss was having one of those seasons of hardship where he was completely unaware his non-work-related issues were contaminating his leadership. He started in on the guy but his employee had enough. He started yelling at the boss including a few choice curse words. He yelled about the bosses' attitude, and how stupid and ineffective he felt after the regular chastising. He said today is my last day because I can't deal with you anymore.

The boss was so taken aback by the response he got from his top employee that he said, "Wait. I'm sorry. What are you talking about." The employee looked at him enraged, and the boss said, "No really, I don't know what you are talking about." The employee's face changed when he realized that his boss was completely clueless. He started to share how incredibly powerful the bosses' behavior and words are. How he was so successful because of his ability to encourage but at the same time, devastatingly hurtful when he was discouraging.

A few months later, we were introduced at a dinner and he began talking about his experience and how he wanted to change but he had no idea what to do. I recommended he take an Emotional Intelligence assessment. He did and it was very telling and also very predictable based on the story he shared at our meeting. It was quite amusing at first, we would laugh together as he realized he was a walking robot that had no concept of emotions. Nor the fact that understanding emotions could be very powerful and helpful.

One of the most fruitful things that came out of our interactions was that he is now open and receptive to feedback. More than that, he has told his team that they can call him out if he is starting to act funny. It is almost like the candy bar commercial where they say, "You should eat something, you get really cranky when you are hungry." His employees were nervous at first, as was the boss. With time and practice, they all got better at giving and receiving feedback both positive and negative.

As a summary; You are not leading anyone if you have no power or influence. Power and influence can be dangerously intoxicating if you are not careful or if you haven't developed the character to contain the responsibility it comes with. Authority inherently can create distance between those who don't have it or it can cause a magnetic draw. You have to be careful who you surround yourself with but you also need to remember to not be afraid to let people in. Emotional Intelligence and openness to correction and accountability are crucial for your success and longevity.

THE LONELINESS OF DECISION

Decision-making is one of the most isolating elements of leadership. As a leader, you are going to make the decisions that affect everyone in your company, or on your team. Sometimes your decisions can cascade and either result in something great or something terrible.

As mentioned in the last chapter, some leaders work in very high-stakes positions. I was watching a TV show the other day with government officials having very important conversations. I watched as the different members of the government had to come up with ways that everyone would be happy, or at the very least avoid world war three. Now I recognize that this is a TV show but there are people in this world who make decisions that carry this much weight. I personally don't ever want to carry that much responsibility. Decisions have consequences no matter what.

As a side note, I want to reclaim the word consequence. It always seems to have a negative connotation attached. Webster calls it "Something produced by a cause or necessarily following from a set of conditions." For example, if you eat well and exercise regularly you will be healthier than if you don't. If you eat garbage and sit on the couch, you will likely be unhealthy in the future. Consequences.

Every choice and every action has a consequence. The greater your level of influence and power the further those consequences reach. The first thing that you probably already know if you are a leader is; Someone is always going to be mad at you for your decision or at least unhappy. There are people who have a genuine interest in the opposite decision you make that affects them financially or otherwise. There will also be haters out there who don't like you, who are unhappy with their lives and will try to take it out on you.

Having accountability is very important in every way to surviving leadership positions, but sometimes oversite can be difficult and take a toll on your mental health. I know someone who is a manager of a large hotel and resorts in Florida. It has many very wealthy unit owners and also renters. There is also a board of directors that she has to report to. She has shared countless stories of being stuck in the middle of the tenants and the board. It is fascinating the difference between those who are wealthy tenants vs. very wealthy tenants. The moderately wealthy people there approach the manager with contempt and arrogance whereas the highly wealthy are far more respectful when making their requests known.

It is my belief that those who are highly wealthy rarely got their completely on their own. They had to have relationships with people to get to the top. They have learned to delegate and so they are generally less stressed out. They also know that being respectful will get you much further in this type of situation. Of course, the resort manager is going to take care of something that is potentially dangerous for example. So all they have to do is let the management know, and request that they take care of it as soon as possible. However, the opposite seems to happen with regard to those who are moderately wealthy. I believe again it has to do with the fact that they are still trying to figure out the significance of the relationship. They may not have learned yet that if you disrespect those who are doing their job, they might just not do their job all that fast.

In the case of my friend, she doesn't just get to do her job in the best way she thinks things should be. She has to figure out how to make it look like things are moving in the right direction at every stage of the project. I know as a project manager that there will be many times when things don't look like they are moving or may look ugly for a moment, but if the wrong person sees it, it could be catastrophic. This is just an additional stress that happens to those in leadership.

You as a leader need to find what brings you life, what restores your energy and mental health. There are times when you will process your thoughts and it can be highly stressful. Or after you have made a decision and you are waiting to see what is going to happen. It is up to you to find a way to take a moment out of the chaos of work to be refreshed. I highly recommend corporate retreats or whatever works for you.

As a leader, you are going to be faced with those who like your idea or decision and those who don't. You need to recognize that this is a part of the job. Finding a way to be able to hear what everyone is saying and consider all suggestions from your trusted advisors. In the end, you are the one who has to make the decision and live with the consequences of not only the decision but also going against those who had contrary objections. Also, a great leader is able to be right and not need to remind people who they are. There may be times when you need to pull someone aside after your idea has worked out and help them to see that their objection was appreciated but perhaps the way they objected wasn't appropriate. However, "I told you so!" is usually quite unaccepted by great leaders.

Another consideration as to why you need to surround yourself with other leaders of great character is that you are responsible for the decisions that you make. I believe that you will stand before God and account for your decisions. If you don't believe that, you must realize to be a great leader, you have to make the right, ethical, moral, or appropriate decision with the information that you have at a given time for your own integrity. No matter what is against you. A great example of an incredibly difficult situation was Abraham Lincoln. We, in the "Modern, civilized" world know that slavery is wrong as well as illegal. However, in Lincoln's day, not only was it legal, but many people saw fiscal benefits, as well as efficient use of those not considered a whole person. People would have argued against his moral and legal arguments with the rule of law on their side. Lincoln and those who were with him, knew it was human decency that dictated the demand for the abolition of slavery in the US. So all that to say, Abraham was literally going against the establishment, something we talk about today but no one is truly doing. He needed great counsel and people by his side.

Abraham Lincoln, the 16th President of the United States, faced one of the greatest challenges in American history: the Civil War. As the nation grappled with the conflict between the North and the South, Lincoln was confronted with the weighty responsibility of leading the country through a time of unprecedented division and strife. In his role as the commander-in-chief, Lincoln was alone in making the final decisions that would determine the fate of the nation and shape the course of history (McPherson, 1988).

One of the most significant decisions Lincoln made during his presidency was the issuance of the Emancipation Proclamation on January 1, 1863. This proclamation declared the freedom of slaves in Confederate territory, marking a pivotal moment in the fight against slavery and laying the groundwork for the eventual abolition of slavery throughout the United States. Lincoln understood the moral imperative of ending slavery and recognized that this decision would have profound consequences for the nation.

Lincoln's decision to issue the Emancipation Proclamation was not without its challenges. He faced opposition from both political and military circles, with some arguing that it would further escalate the war and others questioning the constitutionality of such a measure. Furthermore, slavery was great from a financial profit position. Lincoln could have said thought that slavery is accepted by most and absolutely legal, so why not lean into it and become incredibly rich and have an easy life? However, Lincoln persevered, driven by his unwavering commitment to justice and equality.

The consequences of Lincoln's decision were monumental. The Emancipation Proclamation not only transformed the status of millions of enslaved individuals but also had a profound impact on the course of the Civil War itself. It shifted the focus of the conflict from solely preserving the Union to one that included the abolition of slavery as a central goal. This decision also had far-reaching implications for the future of the United States, setting the stage for the passage of the Thirteenth Amendment to the U.S. Constitution, which formally abolished slavery throughout the country.

Abraham Lincoln's leadership and the weight of the decisions he made during his presidency demonstrate his immense courage, vision, and commitment to the principles of equality and justice. By standing firm in his conviction to end slavery and preserve the Union, he shaped the course of American history and left a profound and lasting impact on the nation.

Lessons learned from the experiences of leaders who made successful decisions in isolation provide valuable guidance for others facing similar challenges. These leaders often demonstrate the importance of maintaining composure, seeking diverse input, and making well-informed decisions based on available information. They emphasize the need to balance assertiveness with humility, showing a willingness to listen and learn from others. Strategies employed by successful leaders include establishing clear decision-making frameworks, fostering a culture of trust and collaboration, and leveraging technology to facilitate communication and consultation.

This is a rare scenario that Lincoln was in. It is common amongst the most, epic historic successes, but also the equally incredible failures. Having great counsel is absolutely necessary in order for a leader to succeed. However, as a leader, there may be times when you have to stand alone, buck the opinions and thoughts of those around you, and go for it. It would be difficult to know the number of times people bet the house on something and it fails because we only hear about the times where it worked. Again, the final decision rests with you so you are the one who needs to not cave to pressure, but rather receive counsel, consider it, and make a decision.

I have heard from many of these inspirational speakers something to the effect of, "Never let them know what you are working on until it's available." This is a complicated minefield to navigate. I believe, "Keep the circle very small until you are ready to share with the world." The paradox that you will face is that there are people who don't want to see you succeed. I don't remember who said it, but it was, "People are fine with you as long as you stay at the level you were at when you met them. As soon as you decide you want to level up, people will start having problems with you." Now this is often but not always true. In the context of a job. Most employees are fine as long as you don't actually change anything. So you need to balance working out your vision with a very small circle at first. Once that vision or idea is more solid, then you can start to expand the circle. If not, you run the risk of someone stepping on your dream and discouraging you enough you may toss the idea.

Finding a way to not share every excitement that you have and maintaining a level of confidentiality with your own things while being open is the balance that you will have to develop with experience.

It is a rare gift for those who are able to stand firm with their decisions in the face of overwhelming opposition. My mom was watching one of those discovery channel shows and she excitedly shared what she had learned about Hershey's company and their history.

Mr. Milton S. Hershey, the founder of Hershey's Chocolate, had an extraordinary vision that caused him to build an entire town dedicated to his employees and their families. This grand project, known as Hershey, Pennsylvania, is a testament to Mr. Hershey's vision and commitment to the well-being of his workforce. Something that I believe all leaders can learn from. Is it necessary to go this far for the care of your workers, probably not, but would it completely change the culture of your company if this was the motivation behind your leadership? Absolutely.

In the early 1900s, Milton Hershey makes incredible strides with his chocolate manufacturing business. Recognizing the importance of providing a nurturing environment for his employees, he decided to create a model community where they could live, work, and thrive. In 1903, construction began on what would become Hershey, Pennsylvania.

The town's development included the construction of employee housing, schools, parks, a community center, and even a hospital. Mr. Hershey believed that he could create a loyal and dedicated workforce by offering affordable, comfortable housing and providing access to education and healthcare. The town was designed to foster a sense of community, with a focus on family values and recreational opportunities.

One of the notable aspects of the Hershey community was the Hershey Industrial School (now known as the Milton Hershey School), which Mr. Hershey founded in 1909. The school provided education and care to orphaned boys, giving them an opportunity for a brighter future. It remains an important part of the Hershey legacy to this day. To think, there was no manipulation or ulterior motives, he simply knew that if he took care of his workers, they would work hard for him.

Here is where things get interesting, in 1937 after Mr. Hershey decided to do everything he could to keep his labor force throughout the Great Depression, his labor force decided that they would go on strike against the company. The company that created an ENTIRE city for them. However, the labor dispute would be shut down when the farmers who provided the milk and other products came out because of the damage it was causing their livelihood.

As an aside, this is one of the things that workers who are not leaders don't see. It is also one of the earmarks of a great leader. Great leaders see that their decisions have a greater impact than what they initially see. A follower sees, "I am going to stop working so the fat cats don't get their money." A great leader says, "I want a raise, but I need to find a way that I can get the raise while everyone wins."

Many of you know that Steve Jobs wore the same outfit every day. It is well known that he did that to avoid having to make the decision of what to wear. There are many documented studies about decision-making fatigue. In summary, you have a finite number of decisions you can make per day based on the decision-making energy you have. A relatable example is the first few weeks after you get a new job. Even if it's a job you are familiar with you will be very drained in those early days. The reason is our brains create programs that take care of unimportant things, such as the route you drive to work, the way from your office to the copy machine, how to use the new coffee maker, etc. When you have learned the pattern to do these things, your brain can autopilot those things to free up decision-making energy for other things. This is why sometimes you don't remember driving home. You were in fact aware of the trip but you didn't have to think about any of the turns or speed limits anywhere because you know them well. Over time depending on your job, you are able to just do the job without having too many decisions to make so you will be less tired.

Now, as a leader, you are constantly inundated with decisions that are sometimes repetitious but often new. This means that you never get to create a pattern to coast on when you need a rest. Decision-making fatigue is a very real issue for everyone, but far more noticeable and problematic for leaders. As we will talk about in probably every chapter, self-care is one of the ways to mitigate some of the burnout and allow you to continue to make effective and healthy decisions. In the final chapter of the book, we will discuss more about what self-care really is. It doesn't have to be sitting at a spa with cucumbers on your eyes, unless of course, that is your definition of self-care.

One of the ways that you can help yourself practically is by using a decision-making framework. Here is a list of a few ideas that you can spend more time researching:
Rational Decision-Making: This traditional framework involves a logical and systematic approach to decision-making. It typically includes steps such as identifying the problem, gathering relevant information, generating alternatives, evaluating options, making a choice, and implementing and evaluating the decision.

Decision Matrix Analysis: This framework involves creating a matrix that compares and evaluates alternatives based on different criteria. Each alternative is assessed against the criteria, and scores or weights are assigned to determine the most suitable option.

Cost-Benefit Analysis: This framework involves comparing the costs and benefits of different options to determine their overall value. It quantifies the potential costs and benefits and considers each alternative's financial, social, and environmental implications.

SWOT Analysis: SWOT stands for Strengths, Weaknesses, Opportunities, and Threats. This framework involves analyzing the internal strengths and weaknesses of an organization or situation, as well as the external opportunities and threats. It helps identify the factors that may influence decision outcomes.

Decision Trees: Decision trees are graphical representations of decision-making processes. They map out different decision paths, possible outcomes, and associated probabilities. Decision trees are particularly useful in situations with multiple sequential decisions and uncertain outcomes.

Six Thinking Hats: This framework, developed by Edward de Bono, involves considering a decision from different perspectives represented by six imaginary hats. Each hat represents a different thinking style (e.g., analytical, creative, emotional), allowing for a more comprehensive exploration of the decision problem.

As you are regularly faced with decisions a couple of skills that you should develop are:

Building self-assurance through experience and learning:
In the leadership decision-making process, building self-assurance is crucial for making effective decisions. Experience plays a significant role in developing confidence and judgment. Leaders who have encountered various situations and learned from their successes and failures are better equipped to make informed decisions. Through experience, they gain insights into what works and what doesn't, which helps them navigate complex decision-making scenarios with greater self-assurance.

Continuous learning also plays a vital role in building self-assurance. Leaders who actively seek new knowledge, stay updated with industry trends, and engage in professional development opportunities enhance their decision-making abilities. They acquire a broader perspective, gather diverse viewpoints, and integrate new insights into their decision-making processes. Learning helps leaders become more adaptable, flexible, and confident in their ability to tackle challenges and make sound decisions.

Leveraging Intuition and Expertise:
In addition to experience and learning, leaders can leverage intuition and expertise in decision-making. Intuition refers to the ability to make judgments and decisions based on instinct or a deep understanding of a situation, even when explicit reasoning is not readily available. Experienced leaders often develop a keen sense of intuition through years of practice and exposure to similar scenarios. They can tap into their intuition to make decisions quickly and effectively, especially in time-sensitive situations where extensive analysis may not be feasible.

Expertise is another valuable asset in the decision-making process. Leaders who have developed expertise in their field have in-depth knowledge and understanding of the relevant factors, best practices, and potential outcomes. They can draw on their expertise to assess situations, identify patterns, and anticipate potential risks or opportunities. Expertise allows leaders to make well-informed decisions based on a solid foundation of knowledge and understanding.

However, it's important to note that intuition and expertise should not replace critical thinking or thorough analysis. They should complement and inform the decision-making process, serving as additional tools for leaders to consider. Effective leaders strike a balance between leveraging their intuition and expertise while also considering available data, conducting analysis, and seeking input from others to make well-rounded decisions. By building self-assurance through experience and learning, and leveraging intuition and expertise, leaders enhance their decision-making capabilities and become more adept at making informed choices that drive positive outcomes for their organizations and stakeholders. One of those paradoxes of leadership: yes do not replace critical thinking and thorough analysis, but at the same time, you most likely have it inside you. Pure coaching involves a person who solely asks questions because as a coach we know that you are more of an expert in the field you work in. My job as a coach in a pure coach setting is to draw out of you the answer that is just covered with other stuff.

Finally, building a professional support network is invaluable for the decision-making process as well as just general support in your professional role. I am still going to discuss what I call a "Life team." We will discuss more on this in a later chapter.

THE LONELINESS OF SACRIFICE

Exploring the personal sacrifices made by leaders also challenges common misconceptions and myths surrounding leadership. It dispels the notion that leadership is solely about power, prestige, and success. Instead, it reveals the hidden sacrifices that leaders willingly make in their pursuit of a vision, the growth of their organizations, and the well-being of their teams. By acknowledging and discussing these sacrifices, we move towards a more comprehensive and nuanced understanding of leadership, beyond the façade of authority and influence. Moreover, there has been this belief that CEOs or leaders of large companies should make the same amount of money as the lowest laborers because it should be equal.

I don't want to dissect every leader out there and discuss what they are getting paid because yes, I do believe that there are some people who are overpaid. That said, no one takes the burden of leadership the way the owner does. From the financial liability, coming up with the idea of the company, the fortitude to make it happen as well as being able to navigate all of the things that I have mentioned so far in this book. So to be clear, I am not for paying the upper management the same salary as the person who tapes boxes closed and puts them on a pallet. I am in favor of making sure management deserves a higher salary and responsibility. I also want to reiterate that all humans are of the same value intrinsically but not all people contribute the same value to society or to an organization.

By understanding the sacrifices leaders make, we are able to have more grace and compassion. Not only for what they are going through but also to understand how our infallible heroes can make a mistake or be offensive. Furthermore based on the perpetuated belief above regarding everyone deserving the same pay, people can evaluate if they are willing to sacrifice so much to be in the higher level role.

There is a bible scripture where it records Jesus saying that He is the good shepherd, and a hired hand will not lay their life down for the sheep only the owner will. This principle applies to businesses or other organizations as well. The company owner will work themselves to the bone to try to make sure a business stays afloat whereas many employees would jump ship before it sinks rather than stick around to try to plug the holes.

Leaders make sacrifices seen and vastly unseen. In my experience, the higher level of the leader, the greater the strain on their family and marriage. The reasons for this are fairly predictable but also extend further than some may think. The demands on a leader's time can often lead to a poor or nonexistent work-life balance. With no work-life balance self-care and finding time to do the things that promote longevity are nearly impossible. To be clear, it doesn't have to be this way and we will be discussing ways to mitigate the stress later but I just want to point out the reality that many leaders face.

There are some self-serving motivations behind wanting to sacrifice for one's leadership role, but often times it is actually a very noble drive behind this excessive amount of work and sacrifice. On the selfish side, some people find their identity in their titles. Some people need to feel powerful in order to feel like a good person or a useful person. Others will pursue being busy so they don't have to answer questions about their quality or performance. Meaning, if everyone sees that the leaders are always busy, then they must be doing all they can. If things are failing it's obviously not their fault. Others feel like they are doing something important if they are always busy, but being busy doesn't mean being productive.

Conversely, many leaders just take their work, mission the goal very seriously. I knew a leader who was overseeing a non-profit food distribution that fed over 500 families. Unfortunately, I slowly watched as the leaders mental health deteriorated because of the burden they carried. There was a dispute between this leader and their superiors as well as other issues with the facility used for the distribution. This person would end up working for 10/12 hours on issues that shouldn't have existed in the first place. They felt that if they didn't fight for what they believed in, 500 families would starve to death. Now as you might guess, this wasn't an accurate assumption because many years later the organization had to shift gears and move to a different location. The families in that city did just fine and found other ways to survive.

This leader actually ended up in the hospital from all the stress. I wish there was something I could have done to change their perspective and remove the weight that they carried. Unfortunately, there are sometimes when people will just believe what they will and you can't fix that. Also, I was quite young and this was before I was really trained on how to coach people into change.

I had a coaching client who worked for a company that had a very unhealthy leadership team. He was a middle-level manager who was fairly fresh out of college. He had contracted me as a coach to help him through some professional hurdles that he was facing. My professional opinion was that he needed to run not walk away from his job. However, he was so committed to the experience and opportunities that he may have because of his time in a mid-level leadership role at this company, he decided to stay for a few years. The toll it took on his energy and health was very concerning, but it was the choice he made.

Success will always take time of unbalance in order to find balance. Not only is that a result of the need for the practice of how to become balanced but also because in order to build it takes times of hard work and times of less work. Having spent over a decade in construction, I have a lot of analogies that deal with building. When you are going to build a house, there will be times of balance and unbalance. Someone will go out to a job site and dig where the foundation needs to be made. Once that is ready, someone creates the form for where the concrete will be poured. These steps can be made at almost any pace within reason. However, once that concrete truck arrives, there is no time to be playing around. The concrete has limited viability. Also, once it's poured, it needs to be finished before it completely sets. If you miss that timing, you either need to do a lot of refinishing work or you need to break the whole thing out and start over. As a leader, there are going to be times, no matter how well you plan, no matter how amazing your team is where your work-life is very unbalanced.

Leading well does require great personal sacrifice. One of the hallmarks of leaders is that they are willing to put the needs of those around them over themselves. One of the characteristics of Great leaders is the ability to have boundaries amidst the almost compulsive need to go after the main goal no matter the cost.

Many years ago, I was a project manager for a general contractor. We were working on a renovation for a major grocery store. This particular phase of the renovation was to turn a storage room into an office. This part of the project happened to fall during the holiday season. The phrase was almost finished, and our company was taking our last day before Christmas week. We did a fun full company scavenger hunt in downtown Honolulu and then we had some dim sum and then were going to take off from lunch since it was Friday. I was very excited as it had been an extraordinarily busy holiday season. If you are unfamiliar with construction projects, organizations will wait 8 months out of the year, hem and haw about decisions, and then want you to finish the project before the end of the year so they can get rid of some of their profit before the calendar year closes. This would be fine if only one or two companies thought they were clever, but unfortunately, sometimes it can be 5-10 or more projects that people want to be done.

As we packed up from lunch and began to say our goodbyes and wish each other Merry Christmas, I get a call from the grocery store liaison, and he asks me why the office hasn't been finished and why there was no one on-site. This particular scenario was that the person who called was responsible for getting our company a lot of work so we had to placate him often. Even in situations like this where he randomly made up a deadline out of the blue that had nothing to do with anything discussed previously. He said he needed the office to be available on Monday.

I asked if any of the crew could work, and one guy with a very disappointed look said he would come in. He was able to do the cabinetry fairly quickly (basically by the end of what would have been a full workday.) However, I learned during a phone call why my air conditioner contractor had not finished his part of the job. He was a very sweet older man who didn't know how to tell me that his crew was not licensed for the very specific unit that was specified for the project. So there I sat, late on a Friday with no one capable of coming to finish the air conditioner in a hot office in Hawaii. I started frantically making phone calls to the AC distributors in Hawaii trying to find out who was able to install this darn thing. Only to learn there were 2 companies in the state able to do so. Both of them were fully booked. I sat there feeling helpless and alone at that moment. I was so overwhelmed with disappointment because I was looking forward to having a little bit of time off. I was tired because of all that I had done that day, and also as a leader, I take full responsibility for projects or things that I have my hand on. So I was feeling like there was no way I would make the deadline and I was losing it. Thankfully I was single so I didn't have a wife or kids that I was going to disappoint as well, but it really gave me perspective on the sacrifices leaders make who do have families.

After a few hours, we reached the very end of the workday, I get a call back from the local distributor. He tells me that he got off the phone with an AC company, and the owner told him, "I know that guy, he is solid. We can't do the job but try to find someone to help him out." Side note, this is why leading with integrity is important. The world is smaller than you would believe (especially if you live on an island!) Turns out, I had hired one of the licensed companies on a project I had worked on a few years prior. Apparently, my treatment of the owner and his employees left enough of an impression that he vouched for me during my crisis. The distributor says that the other licensed contractor will call me and discuss how to make it happen. The AC contractor said that he was going to be working on jobs until 10:00 that night. Then he said that he would come after. This was a miracle, on a Friday someone who was already booked was going to come in and do overnight work based on a verbal agreement. My office was already closed so I couldn't get a check or any other payment method. They just trusted that I would pay them sometime after the weekend.

I went home at around 7:00 Saturday morning. I was so overwhelmed with emotion. I was angry because of the way things played out, but I was also so grateful that a company came to our rescue. That to say, I was not the most friendly person that weekend. Thankfully as I mentioned without a family to experience my wrath, I just sat alone and sulked until I was feeling better. Fortunately, I had Sunday to deal with my emotions and get myself together to not take out any feelings on my crew.

Leaders are often faced with things you couldn't imagine. Did you know that you are the only person who communicates exactly the way you do? This means that you learn a certain way, you have things that upset you, things that energize you, concepts that you understand, and some that you don't. This means that a leader has to do their best to know the best way to communicate with everyone on their team and find a middle ground.

People in leadership roles need to do their job, and then they have to pick up the slack for anyone who didn't do their job. A little extra from one employee than the next can add up to an astonishing amount of work. There are considerations that leaders have that an employee wouldn't even consider. So the cost of our electrical is getting a little high. What if we switched to a more energy-efficient lighting solution? How long would that take to pay itself off? Who can be called to come in and look at this? Can I trust this contractor?

Leaders don't get to clock out most of the time. An employee experiences a sudden death of a loved one. The leader has to be compassionate for the person who just experienced such a horrific event. On the other hand, now the leader has an entire person's workload to figure out what to do with. Yes, the death of the loved one is tragic, it would also be very sad if the company closed because the workload fell through and the company lost its largest contract, and that mourning employee doesn't have a company to come back to. The ability to have boundaries between their professional and personal life is so incredibly difficult.

My latest degree was from Concordia University in Irvine at what's called the Townsend Institute. You will read references to things that Dr. John Townsend has written as well as things from one of the institute fellows, Patrick Lencioni. Both of them have been essential in not only my decision to pursue leadership and coaching but also helped with the vast majority of the tools I utilize when I coach or consult.

As difficult as setting boundaries is, it is absolutely vital for the success of a leader and honestly their survival in the role. Dr.

Townsend has written a vast library of books, I would highly recommend you read his books on professional and personal boundaries. He can far better explain why to have boundaries as well as how to create them.

There are many studies that show when a company promotes and lives out a high level of healthy work-life balance, they are more productive and creative. However, all organizational change and culture come from the top. If you as a leader don't know how to have a work-life balance then your employees or those you lead will feel that it's not something that's acceptable within your organization. When you live it out, and give others the freedom to feel that they are allowed to do the same, you will create a culture that breeds health and productivity.

Developing a team that you can trust to complete tasks is also crucial to being able to not bear the weight of the world by yourself. The sacrifices made can be far less on one individual when everyone takes a small hit for the team. The challenge is to try to demonstrate and motivate people to take ownership of the work that they are doing. This will help employees feel like owners and not just hired hands who can walk away at any moment.

There is a balance that also must be found between success based on traditional metrics and based on other more holistic views of success. This giant philosophical question that most people will wrestle with at some point or another is, "Why am I here?" Personally, as a Christian, I have my belief about becoming more like Jesus and demonstrating love in the world and a few other things. However for you maybe it's something different, whatever it is, you need to have an answer to that question. As you are faced with these very challenging obstacles such as immense loneliness and stress, you need to have a reference point to compare to. Does this stress line up with my life's purpose? The balance must be made between the success of a company financially so that way everyone can stay employed as well as able to continue to provide the product or service. And, you must realize that barring a short list of professional roles such as our soldiers and police, generally, your job shouldn't cost you your life.

Research suggests a correlation between high-level executive roles and heart disease or other stress-related illnesses and death. If you are laying your life down on the sword daily then something needs to change. Other than your ego, there is no reason in today's world to have to live without a supportive team. Those you work with should be selected because they are willing to be part of a team. I know that sounds very derivative, but it's true and often overlooked. We hear people in their interviews talk about wanting to be on a team but are they truly willing to sacrifice their ego, their need to have things go their way to make sure the canoe keeps moving in the same direction? When you find people who are like that, you can create a culture that will be willing to support each other on the team. It should look like the activity that schools used to do in primary school where people stand in a close circle and then all sit down at the same time so they are all sitting on each other's knees.

This means that everyone is supporting everyone. This also means for the moments one person is tired, it doesn't matter because they are all supporting each other. I can make a mistake because someone will catch it. Others can make mistakes as well because someone on the team will be there to help clean up the mess.

As I mentioned, I've worked for some very unhealthy companies in my lifetime. One day I moved over to a company where my direct supervisor was a very family-oriented person. There were a couple of times when I needed to take care of things that were personal. Once it was simply that my mom flew back home early and needed a ride to her house from the airport. I didn't plan for it because she was supposed to land late enough for my sister to pick her up. However my boss didn't just say it was okay, he told me to, "Get my @$$ out of the office and go take care of my mom." Now maybe you don't need to lead with such… Clarity, but making something personal a priority was so powerful for me. Now keep in mind, I was good at my job and on top of things, so even though we were busy, I wasn't dumping a disaster on him by cutting out early for the day. As a result of the respect for me and my family, I wanted to work extra hard to make sure we did well as a team. Another time, my father had a heart attack and it was quite stressful for me. It was a little hard to concentrate when I knew that he was at the hospital. I wasn't able to visit him at the hospital so I decided to just keep working. My boss at the time was very patient with me and he also would check in periodically over the weekend to see how my dad was doing. This is the type of treatment that kept me at the company even in spite of upper management being well, not good at their job.

One final sacrifice that may sound a little strange. Leaders need to sacrifice their desire for vengeance as well as any grudges. There is a well-known quote about unforgiveness that says, "Holding onto unforgiveness is like drinking poison and hoping the other person gets sick." It's well-known and cliché because it is true. There are people who will do you wrong. There are people who will unintentionally hurt you as well as some who will do it intentionally. Holding onto a grudge or trying to get vengeance is very unhealthy.

If you are trying to get your revenge, one day you might get it. You will feel very empty and unsatisfied, and further, if you are effective, you will feel worse because you are above whatever you did. Also, if you are allowing the chip on your shoulder to stick around, you are likely to be the person hurting others around you. Even beyond that, when we have these offenses and hurt that we don't let go of, we build walls to protect us from future hurt but we end up not letting the good and healthy people in.

THE LONELINESS OF VISION

Your job as a leader is to cast vision. However, there are times when you are the only one who can see it. That is a lonely place to be. One great story of a leader who had a vision that people really didn't get behind right away is, Howard Schultz, the former CEO and Chairman of Starbucks.

Howard Schultz joined Starbucks in the 1980s when it was a small coffee shop chain with a limited presence in the United States. However, Schultz had a grand vision to transform Starbucks into a global brand and create a "third place" experience for customers—a place between home and work where people could gather, connect, and enjoy high-quality coffee.

Schultz faced significant resistance and skepticism when he proposed expanding Starbucks beyond its original concept as a coffee bean retailer. Many people doubted the market potential for specialty coffee and questioned whether customers would be willing to pay a premium for a cup of coffee.

Undeterred by the doubts, Schultz took a bold step and left Starbucks to start his own coffeehouse chain called Il Giornale. He focused on creating a unique experience for customers by offering a wide range of coffee beverages, a comfortable ambiance, and knowledgeable baristas.

In 1987, Schultz acquired Starbucks and merged it with Il Giornale, assuming the role of CEO. Under Schultz's leadership, Starbucks underwent rapid expansion and became a global phenomenon. Schultz introduced innovative concepts such as the Starbucks Reserve Roastery and Starbucks Reserve stores, elevating the coffee experience to new heights.

Schultz's vision went beyond just selling coffee; he aimed to create a company with a strong social impact. He prioritized corporate social responsibility, fair trade practices, and employee benefits, establishing Starbucks as a leader in ethical business practices.

Today, Starbucks has thousands of stores worldwide and has become synonymous with premium coffee and a unique customer experience. Schultz's visionary leadership and relentless pursuit of his vision transformed the coffee industry and reshaped consumer behavior, making Starbucks a cultural icon.

Howard Schultz's story highlights the importance of having a clear vision, perseverance in the face of skepticism, and the willingness to take risks. His entrepreneurial spirit and commitment to creating a meaningful customer experience have made a lasting impact on the coffee industry and serve as an inspiration to aspiring business leaders.

A leader's vision serves as the guiding light that illuminates the path toward a desired future. It is a powerful force that inspires and motivates individuals and organizations to strive for greatness. A vision encapsulates the leader's aspirations, values, and purpose, providing a clear direction and sense of purpose for all those involved. It ignites passion, fuels innovation, and creates a sense of shared mission among team members. A leader's vision is the catalyst that propels individuals and organizations beyond their current state and toward a future of possibilities. It has the potential to transform communities, industries, and even the world at large.

As much as possible you want to try to keep the vision very simple and understandable. However, it's not always possible and there may be many steps involved in your vision. When that's the case, it can be very difficult to distill the vision to a manageable level that people are actually interested in being involved in.

There is a very common attitude that if something isn't broken then why try to fix it? The reality is many people on the ground floor can't have the perspective to see why things are the way they are and why they need to change. Furthermore, there are quite often people who do see the need for things to be different but really aren't willing to put in the work that is required to make the change possible.

One of the challenges leaders face is the potential disconnect between their vision and how it is perceived by others. While leaders may have a clear and compelling vision in mind, it is essential to recognize that individuals within the organization or stakeholders outside of it may interpret the vision differently. This disconnect can arise due to varying backgrounds, experiences, values, and perspectives held by different individuals. Leaders need to acknowledge that their vision may not be immediately understood or embraced by everyone. It requires them to be open to feedback, actively listen to different viewpoints, and be willing to adapt their communication approach to bridge the gap between their vision and others' understanding.

Differing perspectives, biases, and preconceived notions can significantly influence how individuals interpret a leader's vision. People bring their own unique backgrounds, beliefs, and experiences to the table, which can shape their understanding and acceptance of a vision. Also, a challenge that may be faced is your own history as a leader. For example, a person constantly says they are on a diet, but there are never any changes in their health. Or someone who says that they are going to start getting to meetings on time but continue to arrive late. It is hard to trust people who constantly provide lip service with no action. Also if you are someone who keeps changing your vision or focus it waters down the value of your latest vision.

Biases, both conscious and unconscious, can lead to misinterpretations or misjudgments of a leader's vision. Preconceived notions and past experiences may create resistance or skepticism toward the proposed direction. It is important for leaders to be aware of these factors and proactively address them to ensure that their vision is accurately understood.

To effectively communicate and align the vision with diverse audiences, leaders can employ several strategies. Firstly, they need to articulate their vision clearly, using language that is accessible and resonates with different individuals. Simplifying complex ideas and using relatable examples such as analogies can help bridge the understanding gap.

Active listening and creating opportunities for dialogue are crucial in understanding others' perspectives and concerns. By engaging in conversations and actively seeking feedback, leaders can address any misconceptions or reservations about the vision and work towards building a shared understanding. Additionally, leaders should tailor their communication approach to different audiences. Recognizing the unique needs, values, and preferences of various groups allows leaders to customize their messaging to increase the relevance and impact of the vision.

One of the significant challenges in the loneliness of vision is managing and aligning divergent perspectives within a team or organization. When individuals come together with their unique backgrounds, experiences, and viewpoints, it is natural for differing perspectives to emerge. These differences can create tensions and complexities in interpreting and aligning with the leader's vision. Leaders need to recognize and understand these challenges, acknowledging that diverse perspectives can enrich the vision by bringing in fresh ideas and alternative viewpoints. However, managing divergent perspectives requires effective communication, active listening, and creating a safe space for open dialogue and respectful debate.

When multiple individuals within a team or organization hold different visions, conflicts, and tensions can arise. These conflicts may stem from contrary goals, strategies, or values. Reconciling different visions can be a delicate and challenging process, requiring leaders to navigate through disagreements and find common ground.

It's crucial for leaders to create a collaborative environment where different visions are respectfully explored and evaluated. By developing a culture of open-mindedness and promoting constructive dialogue, leaders can facilitate the identification of shared objectives and potential synergies between differing visions.

Leaders must balance between staying true to their original vision and embracing collective input and adaptation. While it is important for leaders to provide a clear direction and maintain consistency, they also need to recognize the value of incorporating diverse perspectives and feedback. Great leaders understand that adaptation and evolution of vision can be necessary for its success. They're open to refining their vision based on new insights and emerging opportunities, while still holding onto the core principles and values that underline their original vision.

To achieve this balance, leaders can promote a culture of trust and psychological safety, where people feel empowered to contribute their ideas and challenge existing assumptions. They can actively seek feedback, involve key stakeholders in the decision-making process, and utilize collective intelligence to clarify and adapt the vision while maintaining its heart.

As mentioned a few times throughout this book, you will need to balance the paradigm of seeking counsel and listening to those around you but also deciding what you are going to do and holding to that with everything that you have. Once again, the greatest leaders or most successful businesses were often created by someone who was absolutely bull-headed and did what they knew they could do no matter what others told them. On the other hand…

I was probably about 12 years old when I had a vision. This vision was that I was going to build a hang glider. The only thing is, I had no idea anything about aeronautics or engineering nor did I have any of the remotely appropriate materials. So, I took some 2x4s and cut them up, created a triangle, and then a box attached to the bottom for me to hang inside. Once the frame was built I grabbed a couple of trash bags and created the canopy. Now that the trash bags were stapled to a heavy wooden frame it was time to test it. I climbed up the ladder, carrying my hang glider with great difficulty. However be it God or parental intuition, my dad brought my mom around the corner with a very, "you need to see what your son is doing right now" look about him. In a genius parenting moment, my parents said that when they test out new designs that can be dangerous for someone inside they always use a dummy of some sort. This was back in the days of the crash dummy commercial for every major car brand and for anti-drinking ads. So since I could relate to this idea, I tied a bunch of toys and other things to the hang glider, climbed up the ladder once more, and threw the hang glider off. As I am sure you guessed, it crashed straight to the ground.

The moral of the story in this context is that you need to have people who can see what you are doing and speak into your life. However, the Wright brothers didn't care what anyone said about what could be done with regard to flight. Personally, I didn't want to fly so badly that I continued to pursue the design and create a working hang glider. Honestly, I am not a fan of heights so I have no idea why I was trying to build the death trap. Perhaps the takeaway is that if you have a vision, maybe seek counsel on the way you are going about achieving the vision but not so much on whether or not you should be attempting to reach the vision itself.

In summary, recognizing the potential disconnect, understanding the impact of differing perspectives, biases, and preconceived notions, and employing effective communication strategies are essential for leaders to navigate the challenge of aligning their vision with diverse audiences. By actively addressing these aspects, leaders can bridge the understanding gap, build trust, and foster a shared commitment toward the realization of their vision.

THE LONELINESS OF PERSPECTIVE

Very similar to Vision, leaders have a different perspective. This is due to two major factors; First off, leaders are wired to see specific things, and second, leaders have access to information that many others will not.

The natural inclination of leaders regarding how they view things is both natural and learned over time. My opinion is generally anything can be learned. However, it is true that certain things are natural or some people have something more natural than others.

The natural as well as the learned perspective of leaders is related to the reticular activating system (RAS). It's a fascinating mechanism within our brain that plays a crucial role in our perception and attention. It acts as a filter, selectively processing information and determining what we notice and focus on amidst the overwhelming amount of stimuli in our environment. Understanding the workings of the RAS can provide valuable insights into how we can harness its power to enhance our productivity, motivation, and overall well-being.

Imagine walking into a crowded room filled with people engaged in various activities and conversations. Your brain is bombarded with a plethora of sights, sounds, and sensations. Amidst this sensory overload, the reticular activating system filters out the irrelevant information and brings the salient details to the forefront of your awareness. It acts as a gatekeeper, allowing you to focus on what's important and meaningful to you at that moment. Whether it's the voice of a friend calling your name or an intriguing object in the corner of the room, the RAS directs your attention, guiding your perception and shaping your reality.

The power of the RAS extends beyond mere perception. It also influences our thoughts, emotions, and actions. When we set clear intentions or goals, the RAS acts as a partner in helping us achieve them. It operates on the principle that what we focus on expands. By consciously directing our attention toward our desired outcomes, the RAS becomes attuned to relevant opportunities and resources in our environment. It's like having a personal assistant, constantly scanning the world for information that aligns with our goals. Through this collaboration with the RAS, we can enhance our problem-solving abilities, boost our motivation, and unlock new pathways for growth and success.

As a leader, when you have taught yourself to notice certain things, you will see them where others won't. An example is depending on the work I am doing, especially if I am doing the same thing for a bit, I will begin to notice certain things more than others. When I would work on a small construction project for a friend, I would notice what I was working on, the quality of my work, and how it lines up with the surrounding area. However, if I keep doing small projects for a season, I will begin to notice the construction quality when I am out and about just living my daily life. For example, I may begin to notice poor connections in joints in a small coffee shop. If I visit a friend's house for dinner, I may notice the material that is used in their kitchen and the type of cabinets they have.

Once I was at a friend's house for a get-together, and I noticed they had a full slab of marble on top of their giant kitchen island.

Most houses in Hawaii have much more narrow islands. It was also at a very unique diagonal as compared to the other lines within the kitchen. I mentioned it to the host and he laughed at me. I don't remember the reason they decided to build it the way they did but he thought it was funny that I was the only person to have noticed outside of the people who walked through the kitchen when it was first built many years prior.

I believe there are things that you notice that many people around you do not. That is the result of your RAS. But your perspective is far more than just your ability to notice things, it also directly deals with how you view the world, perhaps as a leader, you notice systems around you. You look and see things that may be frustrating because you see a potential for making things better, smoother, faster, more efficient, or something else. That in and of itself can be the cause of an element of loneliness.

However, it's also more than all of what we have covered so far. As a leader, you have access to things that others don't. You may be hearing about people who take issue with you. They say never read online comments but sometimes we do, and that can be devastating. Perhaps you have learned about something that one of your employees is going through personally and of course, it's something that needs to be kept in confidence. Without someone to process the situation with it can be very difficult.

Maybe you are looking at the financials and are forecasting that if something doesn't change dramatically and soon you are going to have to let employees go. Now you have to look at the people you care for, the people that your company is providing for, and know that they are potentially going to be in personal financial trouble. You want to warn them, but at the same time, things could turn around and if they do, telling them may cause unintended problems. Furthermore, it seems there is a correlation between higher intelligence and people struggling with mental health issues such as anxiety. This is not conclusive and also just an example, not the point; It was explained to me by a mental health professional that a higher level of intelligence allowed for the person to be cognizant of far more data than someone who isn't. As though going through life blissfully unaware was actually a benefit. Leaders who get to see with a greater scope of vision can struggle similarly. Just simply trying to process all this information at once.

I believe there is a greater significance to this than we realize or consider. Fifty years ago the amount of data and awareness a leader had was far more localized. Not at all to say leaders of the past had it easier, no. They had different struggles of their own, the completely unacceptable nature of sharing emotions and issues. None of them had an executive coach to help them. However, with the availability of information, and the ability to expand territory to the entire world, the fact that you can innocently say something and get canceled for it and dozens of other detrimental factors. Trying to be aware of all the emotions we are now being taught to manage, in addition to the previous list, can be highly overwhelming.

I use a lot of construction metaphors because I spent many years in construction from the very bottom to the senior project manager of a general contracting company. Also due to my background in construction, I have also coached contractors as well, hopefully, you still can relate my analogies to your own situation.

There is a big disconnect between the field and the office. They are two completely different worlds in almost every way. This is why there is so often a struggle or even an incompatibility when it comes to having a field person try to make the cross-over into the office. It is a little easier to make the transition the opposite way but still nearly impossible. A project manager has three things to consider, Time, Cost and, Quality. An overly distilled concern that a field worker is, getting the job done and getting paid. A leader within the office is not only concerned with everything that the project manager is concerned with but also balancing all the things that come with running a business. In construction, it is things such as cost, profit, reputation, and upcoming work. The better the field worker, or leader, the more things they will be considering. Field workers will begin to be more aware of the schedule and cost overruns, whereas a leader in the office will be paying attention to employee concerns as well as the company.

When leader looks at a project, they are considering if they will make enough money to keep the company going. A leader is looking at scheduling from the perspective of budget and enough hours to retain a field worker, while a worker is looking at the schedule based on having enough hours to survive. A field worker may drag their feet on a project out of fear that the company won't have upcoming work and so if they take their time they will have work until the next project starts. They won't consider the vast ramifications of their actions.

First off they will cost the project money that wasn't planned for. The estimator thought something would take 3 hours, but the employee dragged it out to 8. Money is immediately lost. The following project may get pushed up or back so the future schedule is not up to the field worker. But the leader does need to keep that project schedule in mind. If the worker keeps dragging the schedule the estimator will make adjustments and then they may price themselves out of future projects. Which in turn means that there is truly no work for the worker. Now the leaders have to carry the hardship that they have to let employees go.

The world of a leader and those they lead are very different.

Again a disclaimer, you don't have to believe in anything miraculous or in the Bible itself. The characters who are written about are also found in non-biblical historical texts recording the stories and exploits of these ancient people. Great lessons of leadership can be learned from their lives.

Nehemiah, a prominent figure in the Bible, played a crucial role in the rebuilding of the walls of Jerusalem during a time of great distress and adversity. The story of Nehemiah begins with him serving as the cupbearer to King Artaxerxes of Persia. One day, Nehemiah received news about the broken walls of Jerusalem, which left the city vulnerable and its inhabitants in a state of despair.

Deeply moved by this revelation, Nehemiah sought God's guidance and developed a heartfelt burden to restore the city's walls and bring hope back to its people. With the king's permission, he embarked on a journey to Jerusalem, equipped with resources and a vision to rebuild.

Upon his arrival, Nehemiah faced numerous challenges and opposition from adversaries who opposed the rebuilding efforts. However, with unwavering determination and strong leadership, he rallied the people of Jerusalem, inspiring them to join hands in the monumental task ahead. Nehemiah organized the inhabitants into different groups, each responsible for a specific section of the wall, fostering a sense of unity and shared purpose.

Despite facing external threats and internal conflicts, Nehemiah's leadership, coupled with the people's resilience, prevailed. They worked tirelessly, day and night, with tools in one hand and weapons in the other, always ready to defend against their enemies. Nehemiah's strategic planning, problem-solving skills, and ability to motivate the people ensured steady progress and kept the vision alive.

In the face of adversity and discouragement, Nehemiah encouraged the people to trust in God's provision and remain focused on their mission. Through his steadfast faith and commitment, he demonstrated that rebuilding the walls was not just a physical endeavor but a spiritual one as well.

Ultimately, the walls of Jerusalem were rebuilt, symbolizing the restoration of the city's strength, security, and identity. Nehemiah's leadership and resilience not only transformed the physical landscape but also revitalized the people's faith and sense of community.

The story of Nehemiah serves as a powerful example of a leader who faced overwhelming challenges, yet remained resolute in his purpose. His unwavering determination, strategic approach, and ability to rally others around a common goal are enduring lessons in leadership and the power of perseverance.

Perhaps you don't believe in having a commission from God but I ask if you have a mission in your life. Nehemiah was the cupbearer for the most powerful man on earth at the time. A cupbearer was one of the most trusted roles you could have as a leader. In ancient times, poison was a popular way to try to assassinate a leader. A cupbearer was the person who would taste all of your food and drink before you did so that way you would know if it were safe. If the cupbearer wanted you dead then there was nothing to keep you safe, thus the cupbearer's role was one of great trust. This would also mean that Nehemiah had access to the highest level of military reports, he would have learned about military strategy all the while he would have likely been taught about his people's home in Jerusalem in his home.

He knew what the dangers of a city with no protection at that time would be. King Artaxerxes was quite a conqueror of the time, so he would have witnessed the horrors that befell anyone who was unprotected. Yet as he went to rebuild the wall there were people trying to stop him. I believe that some of them were worried about what King Artaxerxes would think about their actions. Are the Jewish people planning on revolting? Why do the Jewish people need protection, are they not happy with the protection of the King? However, Nehemiah was in the presence of the King and given direct permission as well as help to build the wall. Those on the ground don't often have all the information. At the same time, leaders need to put aside their egos as well and be willing to hear what those on the ground are saying.

I remember a story that I have found many different versions of online and cannot find the origin but it goes something like this. A commander of a large navy destroyer sees a light up ahead. He goes on the radio and says, "Approaching vessel this is navy commander Smith, change course." Then after a few moments a voice responds on the radio and says, "Commander Smith, you change course immediately." Annoyed the commander gets back on the radio and says, "Do you have any idea who I am?" The voice on the radio responds, "You're commander James, and you need to change course immediately." The commander responds furiously yelling, "I am a rear admiral commanding a destroyer, who in God's name do you think you are? Change course!"

The voice on the radio replies, "I am the lighthouse operator."

There will be people out in the field, in your warehouse, and on the factory floor who will have access to information as well. The loneliness of the excess of information for leaders comes from when they are told about the countless things that are going on from many different sources about things that are happening. If we never consider the information that is presented to us as leaders by those who are more involved with the day-to-day we may find ourselves in great trouble.

As I write this book I have been thinking about a friend who I hope is doing well these days. His circumstance was one of the reasons I wanted to write this book. As I feel burdened with perspective which feels very isolating. Around 10 years ago, I was meeting with this man whom I will call David. David was so isolated and alone it was painful to hear him speak. He was so closed up about the things that were going on in his life and his past that it was as though I was the only one on the earth. He didn't believe that he could share his struggles with his staff or his congregation. I offered professional counsel and even offered the name of a few mental health professionals. None of which he was willing to accept. He carried the belief that for sure word would get back to his people and they would reject him, and he would lose everything. I tried to explain that a professional would be as confidential as I am but he only trusted me because I was there for a lot of the trauma he experienced.

Unfortunately, after a couple of years of trying to get through to him, he retreated into himself. Left the ministry, quit his professional job, and cut off all his relationships. There are a few burdens that I carry from this, I have realized that no matter how hard I try as a leader, friend, coach, pastor, or any other relationship, not everyone is willing to change and some may not ever find the relief that they need. The next thing, I desperately want to see is leaders not struggling with such a maddening issue – Loneliness. Especially because loneliness is almost always derived from the desire to grow and help those around them.

In other words, as I write this book, I begin to feel alone or maybe a little helpless thinking, "If only I could have written this book 20 years ago and hopefully helped 20 years' worth of leaders who have been struggling with feeling isolated." As a leader, I thankfully have a life-team and professional team whom I can discuss these feelings with. It doesn't change the fact that I feel this affliction in my soul because of the hurt some leaders are feeling at this moment. Perspective, having greater awareness, or access to greater data can be very isolating.

THE LONELINESS OF FAILURE

The pursuit of success knows no boundaries; it is a timeless desire that resonates with people from all walks of life. Whether we are in bustling cities or remote villages, success is a goal that unites us in our collective human experience. We all strive to create a life that reflects our dreams, passions, and aspirations. From the ambitious entrepreneur yearning to build an empire to the artist seeking recognition for their creative expressions, the universal drive for success fuels our determination and propels us forward.

What makes the pursuit of success so universal is the intrinsic human need for growth and fulfillment. It is a fundamental part of our nature to seek progress and transcend our limitations. Success represents the realization of our potential, the embodiment of our dreams, and the manifestation of our hard work. It is an expression of our unique talents and abilities and a testament to our resilience and perseverance. Regardless of our cultural backgrounds or the paths we choose, the goal of success connects us in our shared quest for a purposeful and meaningful existence.

On the opposing side is the fear of failure. The fear of failure is a powerful force that can grip our hearts and paralyze our actions. It lurks in the depths of our minds, whispering doubts and insecurities, and casting shadows of uncertainty over our endeavors. It is the nagging voice that questions our abilities magnifies our shortcomings, and fills us with apprehension. The fear of failure stems from our innate desire to succeed, to be recognized and admired. We fear the consequences of falling short of our own expectations and the judgments of others. It is a fear born out of vulnerability, of exposing our weaknesses and facing the possibility of rejection or disappointment. Yet, the irony lies in the fact that it is often the fear of failure itself that holds us back from reaching our true potential, trapping us in a cycle of self-doubt and missed opportunities. Embracing the fear of failure, understanding its grip on our lives, and finding the courage to push past it is a transformative journey that opens doors to growth, resilience, and ultimately, success.

The90 loneliness that engulfs leaders after experiencing failure is a heavy burden to bear. In the aftermath of setbacks and disappointments, leaders often find themselves standing alone amidst the wreckage of their aspirations. The weight of responsibility rests heavily on their shoulders as they grapple with the consequences of their decisions. The world seems to grow quieter, as once-trusted allies and supporters retreat into the shadows, leaving the leader to confront their failures in solitude. The isolation intensifies as they navigate the intricate web of emotions, self-doubt, and self-reflection that accompanies failure. It is in these moments that the leader's true character is tested, as they must summon the strength to confront their mistakes, learn from them, and rise above the ashes. The path to redemption is lonely and treacherous, but it is through this solitude that leaders find the opportunity for self-discovery, growth, and resilience to face future challenges. The journey of a leader after failure is a transformative one, marked by introspection, humility, and the determination to rebuild and succeed once again.

In our society, success is often narrowly defined, etched deep into our societal construct. We're bombarded with images and narratives that depict success as a linear journey, marked by predetermined milestones and external symbols of achievement. The traditional measures of success, like wealth, fame, and power, become the yardsticks by which individuals are judged. Society perpetuates this idea that climbing the corporate ladder, amassing material possessions, and garnering societal acclaim are the ultimate benchmarks of success.

But this confined definition fails to acknowledge the multitude of paths success can take. It disregards the beauty of individuality and the varied aspirations and goals people hold. Success isn't a one-size-fits-all concept, and by restricting it to a narrow framework, we stifle creativity, hinder personal growth, and discourage individuals from pursuing their unique passions and dreams.

True success should be viewed as a deeply personal and subjective pursuit. It resides in reaching one's full potential, aligning with personal values, and pursuing meaningful goals that resonate with our inner calling. It encompasses finding joy, contentment, and purpose in our endeavors, irrespective of external validation or material accumulation. Society's narrow definition of success fails to recognize the significance of personal well-being, mental and emotional health, and the positive impact individuals have on their communities and relationships.

It's crucial for us to challenge and redefine society's limited understanding of success. By embracing a more inclusive and holistic perspective, we can celebrate the diverse paths people embark upon to find fulfillment and acknowledge the multitude of achievements that contribute to a rich and meaningful life. True success lies in the freedom to define and pursue our own distinct visions of a purposeful and rewarding existence.

However, we also must remember that if we are working for a person or organization, if they have set our target, we must in fact be aiming for those and meeting those requirements. As shared in previous chapters, we must be honest with ourselves and not just make up our own metrics. We can adjust our attitude regarding the outcome but we still must be aware of the definition of success regarding a project.

Even exceptional leaders are not immune to the impact of social media. It acts as a double-edged razor, far more dangerous than a sword. The power of social media has built entire careers out of seemingly mundane activities, a feat that would have been unimaginable two decades ago. However, this digital landscape has also brought about concerning statistics regarding mental health and overall life satisfaction. The concept of comparison has exponentially intensified. It has evolved from simple observations like, "My neighbor just purchased the latest car or high-tech kitchen appliance," to a more concerning dynamic where strangers, whom we know nothing about, share pictures from exotic locations. Despite our lack of knowledge about the authenticity of these images or the financial background of these individuals, we find ourselves succumbing to jealousy and constructing an entire belief system around their portrayal of success.

What defines failure can be a gray area. Robert Jermain Thomas was a Welsh missionary who played a significant role in introducing Christianity to Korea in the 19th century. Born on February 1, 1839, in Rhayader, Wales, Thomas grew up in a devout Christian family and developed a strong sense of religious calling. He trained at the Presbyterian College in Carmarthen, Wales, and later joined the London Missionary Society (LMS) in 1862.

In his missionary work, Thomas was particularly drawn to East Asia and felt a calling to bring Christianity to the people of Korea. He embarked on a journey to Korea in 1865, facing numerous challenges and dangers along the way. At the time, Korea was a closed society that had strict measures against the entry of foreigners and the spread of foreign religions.

Thomas arrived in Korea in 1866, disguised as a Korean and carrying Bibles written in Chinese characters. He distributed these Bibles secretly, often at great personal risk. Unfortunately, his efforts were discovered by Korean authorities, and on September 20, 1866, he was arrested and executed in Pyongyang, the capital of present-day North Korea.

While Thomas's life was cut short, his death had a profound impact on the spread of Christianity in Korea. His martyrdom and the seeds he planted through his missionary work inspired others to continue his mission. Today, Thomas is recognized as one of the pioneers of Christianity in Korea, and his legacy lives on through his strong Christian presence in the country.

The legend is that an important official got a hold of the Bibles that Jermain had brought with him. The officer noticed the quality of the paper was very high. He decided to use it as wallpaper for his house. One day he began to read what was literally now written on the wall. As he read, he found faith in Jesus and people began descending upon his house to read the "words of life" that were found on this man's wall.

A friend recently shared this story and the most fascinating thing was he described how his first thought was, "If I were the missionary I would have felt like such a failure, my one job, was to share the Bible with the Korean people and I died before it happened."

As leaders, sometimes we are so singularly focused that we may miss what Bob Ross called, "Happy accidents." Just because we didn't reach a target or goal, doesn't mean we can't learn from it or pick up the pieces and make something new and perhaps even better.

In my journey as a leader, I have come to understand the profound value of learning from mistakes and embracing them as opportunities for growth. Mistakes are not mere setbacks or failures; they are valuable lessons that shape our character and refine our leadership abilities. It is through these moments of missteps and errors that we gain valuable insights, uncover hidden weaknesses, and discover the areas we can improve.

When we approach mistakes with an open mind and a willingness to learn, we open ourselves up to transformational growth. It is crucial to cultivate a growth mindset that views mistakes as stepping stones toward success rather than stumbling blocks that hinder our progress. Each mistake becomes an invitation to reflect, analyze, and adapt our strategies, ultimately leading us toward greater wisdom and resilience.

One of the key aspects of learning from mistakes is the willingness to take ownership and responsibility. It requires humility and self-awareness to acknowledge our errors and their impact on others. Instead of shying away from mistakes or placing blame on external factors, true growth comes from embracing accountability and actively seeking ways to rectify the situation. It is through this process of reflection and course correction that we can emerge stronger and more capable as leaders.

Moreover, learning from mistakes is not a solitary endeavor. It involves seeking feedback, seeking the perspectives of others, and fostering a culture of continuous improvement within our teams. By creating an environment where mistakes are seen as opportunities for growth rather than grounds for judgment, we encourage open dialogue, collaboration, and shared learning. This collective approach allows us to harness the collective wisdom of our team members and leverage their diverse experiences to propel our growth as leaders.

Embracing these opportunities for learning, taking ownership of our errors, and fostering a culture of continuous improvement are essential elements of personal and professional development. By cultivating a mindset that embraces mistakes as valuable teachers, we can transform setbacks into stepping stones and grow into stronger, more resilient leaders.

A very famous story of failure is the story of Alexander Fleming. Fleming was a Scottish biologist and pharmacologist. In 1928, while working at St. Mary's Hospital in London, Fleming made a significant mistake that ultimately led to one of the most groundbreaking medical discoveries in history.

Fleming was conducting research on bacteria when he accidentally left a petri dish uncovered for several days. Upon returning to his laboratory, he noticed that mold had grown on the dish and appeared to have killed the surrounding bacteria. Instead of discarding the contaminated culture, Fleming examined it more closely and discovered that the mold, later identified as Penicillium notatum, produced a substance that inhibited bacterial growth.

Realizing the potential significance of his mistake, Fleming continued to investigate the mold's properties and conducted further experiments. His accidental discovery laid the foundation for the development of penicillin, the first widely used antibiotic, which revolutionized the field of medicine and saved countless lives.

It may not seem like much, but any scientist who works with infectious diseases will tell you the potentially catastrophic result of leaving a living culture sitting out on a table. However, Fleming's ability to recognize the opportunity within his mistake and his perseverance in exploring its potential applications exemplify the power of turning setbacks into success. His accidental discovery not only transformed the field of medicine but also paved the way for the development of numerous life-saving antibiotics and shaped modern healthcare practices.

Had I been in Fleming's position I may have responded differently. Sometime nearly 20 years ago, I was working as a manager at a restaurant that had an all-flair bar. This meant that our bartenders flipped the bottles and did tricks, setting things on fire and such. So for fun and because I like to have a working knowledge and basic ability of things that the people I lead need to do, I decided to learn how to blow fire. There are very specific things that you do to be safe. First thing, use a wet towel to wipe any excess alcohol from your face before lighting the flame. Second thing, be mindful of what type of alcohol you are using, this will determine how close you want to hold the flame to your face.

At one family party, I was done for the night and had packed up most things. My sister's boyfriend came late and was asking if I could do it one last time. I figured why not. I had put away most of the things such as the wet rag, so I just decided I would use the bottom corner of my shirt. I started to record on my camera as I would often do. I took a shot of alcohol and made a very bad mistake. I was using the strong stuff, which meant I needed to hold the flame away from my face, I did not. The next thing I know, my face is on fire, so I quickly spit out the remaining alcohol which oddly caught fire too. Normally you need to spit the alcohol out in a very specific way in order for it to catch fire. I was able to put myself out very quickly. However, we were all at my mom's house, so I ran over to the camera to delete the video so she wouldn't kill me.

I watched the video once before deleting it and realized my shirt was on fire and I wiped my face. My face had no mustache and eyebrow in one small spot where the fire went straight up from my face. Was that a failure? Yes, it was. Was it dangerous? Absolutely. Is it funny now? Sure. Here is where I missed the chance to make it into a success. This was in the very first years of online video sharing. There was a website that came out right about the same time called YouTube. If I wasn't so hopped up on adrenaline and fear of my mother, I would have not deleted the video and maybe made some money off of it.

Fleming's story serves as a reminder that mistakes, when

approached with curiosity, open-mindedness, and a willingness to explore new possibilities, can lead to extraordinary breakthroughs and unexpected successes. It highlights the importance of embracing setbacks as opportunities for growth and innovation, ultimately contributing to the advancement of society as a whole.

By creating an environment where our employees are allowed to fail and grow, you create a safety net for people's attempts at creativity. By being willing to lead the charge unafraid to risk and experience failure, you open up the door even further for the confidence of pioneering new ways of doing things. Another thing that results from our willingness to fail is the mitigation of targeting failure. One of my hobbies is archery, I wouldn't consider myself great, but I have fun shooting arrows at the target. Archery is very similar to aiming for anything else. You aim at the target and you go. However, a very common human trait is to aim for what has our focus.

Have you ever seen videos on the internet or in movies where a person puts their hand on a dart board and then the person throwing the dart hits the center of the other person's hand? This is because the person throwing had one thought in mind, "Don't hit my friend's hand." They didn't think to themselves, "I need to hit that bullseye."

Another example of this is, I have coached many people who have said something to the effect of, "I promised I would never be like my mom, dad, boss (insert whoever here). And here I am, being just like them." The reason is they have told themselves their whole lives or however long they have witnessed the person's behaviors, "Whatever you do, don't do, _____." As a result of their focus and energy they spend on not being the thing, they are targeting that behavior. This is why professional athletes spend so much time visualizing winning rather than losing. When we are focused on succeeding and being unafraid to fail, we are far less likely to fail as a byproduct.

THE LONELINESS OF RESISTANCE:
DEALING WITH IMMOVABLE PEOPLE

In the journey of leadership, change is often an inevitable companion. It presents itself in various forms, challenging the status quo and pushing us to evolve and adapt. However, change can be met with resistance, and within that resistance lies a unique form of loneliness. It is the loneliness of resistance, a chapter that delves into the complexities of leading individuals who are resistant to change.

There is a multifaceted nature of resistance and its profound impact on both leaders and their teams. We delve into the emotions and experiences that arise when faced with opposition and the profound sense of isolation that can accompany it. I aim to uncover the underlying reasons behind the resistance and provide strategies for effectively navigating this lonely terrain.

Resistance to change often stems from fear, uncertainty, and a deep-rooted attachment to the familiar. We explore the psychological barriers that prevent individuals from embracing new ideas and perspectives and the consequences this resistance can have on organizational growth and innovation.

I hope not to just document the challenge but also to create a guide, offering practical insights and approaches for leading through resistance. Using the power of empathy, active listening, and effective communication in bridging the gap between leaders and those resistant to change.

As we go through the hurdles of resistance, we recognize that it is not an issue to be feared but rather an opportunity for growth and transformation. By understanding the underlying motivations and addressing the core concerns of those resistant to change, leaders can pave the way for collaborative solutions and foster a culture of adaptability and resilience.

To start, I want to talk about the root of change resistance. In the Heath brothers' brilliant books, we delve into the objection to change and unravel its complexities. Building upon their insightful perspectives on human behavior and decision-making, particularly in their books, "Switch: How to Change Things When Change Is Hard" and "Made to Stick: Why Some Ideas Survive and Others Die," we gain profound insights into the objections people often raise when confronted with change.

One objection that resonates strongly is the fear of the unknown. Change disrupts our comfortable routines and introduces an unsettling sense of uncertainty. It's no surprise that we instinctively recoil from the unfamiliar and resist venturing into uncharted territories. This fear of the unknown becomes a formidable barrier, hindering our ability to embrace change and explore new possibilities.

Another objection stems from the perceived losses or sacrifices that change entails. As the Heath brothers aptly emphasize, we need to address the fundamental question: "What's in it for me?" When individuals feel they must relinquish something they value, whether it's a cherished routine, established status, or even personal relationships, they become resistant to change. To overcome this objection, it becomes imperative to acknowledge and address these perceived losses, reassuring individuals that the benefits and opportunities that accompany change outweigh any sacrifices.

Inertia, the powerful force of maintaining the status quo, is yet another objection the Heath brothers shed light upon. It's human nature to stick with what is familiar and comfortable, avoiding the exertion and uncertainty that change often demands. Overcoming this objection requires crafting a compelling case for change, effectively highlighting the rewards and possibilities it offers, and providing individuals with a clear roadmap to navigate the transition.

The Heath brothers also emphasize the significant role emotions play in the objection to change. Change can trigger a multitude of emotions, such as fear, resistance, and skepticism. Recognizing and validating these emotions allows leaders to address them with empathy and understanding, fostering an environment where individuals feel heard, supported, and ultimately motivated to embrace change.

Specifically, the Heath brothers present a powerful metaphor known as the "Elephant and Rider." This metaphor offers a profound understanding of human behavior and provides valuable insights into how to facilitate change effectively.

According to the Heath brothers, the human mind consists of two components: the rational, analytical part referred to as the "Rider," and the emotional, instinctual part likened to the "Elephant." The Rider represents our conscious, logical thinking, while the Elephant symbolizes our unconscious, emotional drives. Understanding the dynamics between these two components is crucial for creating successful change.

The metaphor suggests that the Rider, with its rationality and planning abilities, acts as the director, guiding the Elephant toward a desired destination. However, the Elephant, being significantly larger and more powerful, can easily overpower the

Rider's attempts if it feels uncertain, threatened, or overwhelmed. To achieve effective change, it is essential to address both the rational and emotional aspects, aligning them in a harmonious partnership. By appealing to the Elephant's emotions and providing a clear path for the Rider to follow, change becomes more manageable and likely to succeed.

This concept of the "Elephant and Rider" provides a powerful framework for leaders and change agents. By understanding the motivations, fears, and desires of both the rational and emotional sides, they can develop strategies that engage and motivate individuals on multiple levels. Through careful guidance, shaping the environment, and tapping into people's intrinsic motivations, leaders can influence the Elephant while providing a clear roadmap for the Rider, enabling them to work together toward successful change.

This is one of the practical reasons that I talk so much about leading with empathy and being able to connect with people on an emotional level. Leading with empathy is a transformative approach that has the power to inspire, motivate, and connect with people on a deeper level. It goes beyond simply understanding someone's emotions; it involves putting oneself in their shoes, genuinely listening, and responding with compassion and understanding. Empathy allows leaders to create an inclusive and supportive environment where individuals feel valued, heard, and empowered to contribute their best.

Empathetic leaders recognize the importance of emotional intelligence and its impact on building strong relationships. They have the ability to sense and understand the emotions of others, allowing them to respond in a way that acknowledges and validates those feelings. By actively listening and seeking to understand different perspectives, empathetic leaders create an atmosphere of trust and psychological safety, encouraging open dialogue and collaboration.

Moreover, leading with empathy goes beyond surface-level understanding. It requires leaders to delve deeper into the experiences, challenges, and aspirations of their team members. By demonstrating empathy, leaders show genuine care for their employees' well-being, not just as professionals but as individuals with unique stories and circumstances. They take the time to build meaningful connections and establish rapport, which in turn cultivates a sense of belonging and loyalty among team members.

Leading with empathy also involves considering the impact of decisions and actions on others. Empathetic leaders are mindful of the consequences their choices may have on individuals and strive to make decisions that prioritize collective welfare. They take into account the diverse needs and perspectives of their team, seeking win-win solutions that support both organizational goals and individual growth. By incorporating empathy into their leadership approach, these leaders foster a culture of empathy within their teams, empowering individuals to support and uplift one another.

When we create this environment of safety, we perpetuate the "For you" stance that a leader should maintain where a person can trust that the leader's decisions are always the best they can be for everyone involved. By connecting with people and understanding their emotional responses to things, you can help to move the elephant and not just the rider.

Healthy and productive communication can be key to moving things forward and breaking past difficult resistance. Some tools that you can utilize are:

1. Active Listening: Active listening is a fundamental communication technique that involves fully engaging with the speaker and giving them your undivided attention. This means avoiding distractions, maintaining eye contact, and showing genuine interest in what the

person is saying. By actively listening, you demonstrate respect, understanding, and a willingness to connect with others on a deeper level.

2. Clarification and Reflection: Effective communication involves ensuring that you understand the message accurately. One helpful technique is to clarify and reflect on what the speaker has said. This involves paraphrasing their words and reflecting them back to ensure that you have interpreted their message correctly. It shows that you are actively engaged in the conversation and committed to understanding the speaker's perspective.

3. Empathetic Responding: Responding with empathy is an essential communication technique that helps create a supportive and understanding environment. Empathetic responding involves acknowledging the speaker's emotions and demonstrating understanding and compassion. By validating their feelings and providing a safe space for expression, you foster trust and open communication.

4. Nonverbal Communication: Nonverbal cues play a significant role in effective communication. Pay attention to your body language, facial expressions, and tone of voice. Ensure that your nonverbal signals align with your words to convey sincerity, openness, and attentiveness. A warm smile, nodding in agreement, and maintaining an open posture can enhance your communication and create a positive connection.

5. Clear and Concise Language: Using clear and concise language is vital to ensure that your message is easily understood. Avoid jargon, complex terms, or unnecessary details that may confuse or overwhelm the listener. Instead, strive for simplicity and clarity in your communication, focusing on delivering your message in a way that is accessible and easily digestible.

6. Empowering Questions: Asking empowering questions is a powerful communication technique that encourages dialogue, critical thinking, and problem-solving. Instead of simply providing solutions or directives, ask open-ended

questions that stimulate reflection and invite the speaker to share their ideas and perspectives. This promotes engagement and empowers individuals to take ownership of their thoughts and actions.

7. Respectful Feedback: Providing feedback in a respectful and constructive manner is essential for effective communication. Offer specific and actionable feedback that focuses on behaviors and outcomes, rather than personal attacks. Use a supportive tone and language that encourages growth and development. Remember, feedback should be a two-way process, so be open to receiving feedback as well.

In the journey of leading change, it is crucial for leaders to recognize and address the common barriers that individuals may face when confronted with change. One such barrier is the fear of the unknown. Change often brings uncertainty and the unfamiliar, which can trigger anxiety and resistance. To overcome this barrier, leaders must proactively address concerns and provide clear communication about the change process. By offering information, setting realistic expectations, and highlighting the potential positive outcomes, leaders can help alleviate fear and create a sense of confidence and security among those affected.

Another significant barrier to change is the loss of control. People naturally seek stability and autonomy in their lives, and when faced with change, they may perceive it as a threat to their control and authority. Leaders can overcome this barrier by involving individuals in the change process. By soliciting their input, allowing them to contribute ideas, and providing opportunities for involvement, leaders empower individuals to regain a sense of control and ownership. Additionally, offering support and resources, such as training or mentoring programs, can help individuals develop new skills and increase their confidence in navigating the change. By addressing the loss of control, leaders can foster a sense of empowerment and engagement, promoting a more positive and receptive attitude toward change.

Lastly, skepticism is another common barrier that leaders must navigate when implementing change. Some individuals may question the need for change or doubt its potential benefits. To overcome this barrier, leaders can showcase the value and advantages of the proposed change. This can be achieved by providing real-life examples, case studies, or success stories from other organizations or individuals who have already undergone similar changes. By presenting tangible evidence and highlighting the positive outcomes, leaders can help shift skepticism toward acceptance and enthusiasm for the change.

Overcoming barriers to change requires leaders to identify and address common obstacles such as fear of the unknown, loss of control, and skepticism. By offering strategies such as clear communication, involvement, support, and showcasing the benefits of change, leaders can create an environment that encourages openness, acceptance, and resilience in the face of change. By proactively addressing these barriers, leaders pave the way for successful change implementation and foster a culture of growth and adaptability within their organizations.

To help someone who is resistant to change feel a part of the transition, it's essential to involve them and provide opportunities for active participation. Here are a few strategies I have employed:

1. Open dialogue: Initiate a conversation with the individual to understand their concerns, perspectives, and reservations about the change. Actively listen to their feedback without judgment or defensiveness. This creates a safe space for them to express their thoughts and allows you to address their specific concerns.
2. Seek their input and involvement: Involve the resistant individual in the change process by seeking their input and

ideas. By actively involving them in decision-making and problem-solving related to the change, you empower them to contribute their expertise and insights. This not only helps them feel valued and respected but also gives them a sense of ownership in the transition.

3. Offer training and support: Identify the skills or knowledge gaps that may be contributing to their resistance to change. Provide training opportunities or resources that can help them develop the necessary skills to adapt to the new circumstances. Additionally, offer ongoing support through coaching, mentoring, or peer support programs to assist them in navigating the change successfully.

4. Find a suitable role or responsibility: Explore ways to incorporate the individual into the change process by finding a role or responsibility that aligns with their strengths, interests, and expertise. This can be a specific task, project, or even a leadership role within the transition team. By assigning them a meaningful role, you give them a purpose and a sense of contribution, which can help alleviate resistance and foster their commitment to the change.

5. Recognize and celebrate their contributions: Acknowledge and appreciate the individual's efforts and contributions throughout the change process. Publicly recognize their achievements and the positive impact they have made. This recognition serves as an affirmation of their value and helps them feel acknowledged and included in the overall success of the transition.

One of the last things I would recommend is to celebrate the success without an "I told you so" attitude. People don't need to have their fears rubbed in their faces but be reminded that there is a variation between their feelings and reality. This be helpful in order to perpetuate positive thinking about future endeavors. Also when you are regularly celebrating success you can help to create more bonds between you and your employees thereby reducing the isolation that we feel as leaders.

Internal struggles can contribute to a sense of loneliness. One of the significant sources of resistance we encounter resides within ourselves. This internal resistance stems from deep-rooted beliefs, fears, and insecurities that hinder our ability to lead with confidence and conviction.

At the core of this internal resistance lies the fear of failure and the fear of the unknown. We may question our own capabilities, doubting whether we have what it takes to lead effectively. These self-doubts can lead to a constant battle within ourselves, causing us to hesitate, second-guess our decisions, and shy away from taking risks. The weight of responsibility can be overwhelming, and the fear of making mistakes or being judged by others adds to the burden.

Moreover, our own insecurities and self-limiting beliefs can fuel the resistance within us. We may struggle with imposter syndrome, feeling like we don't deserve our leadership position or that we are not qualified enough. This inner dialogue can create a constant sense of unease, making us question our own worthiness and competence. The loneliness of leadership emerges as we grapple with these internal struggles in solitude, unable to fully share our vulnerabilities with others.

To overcome these difficulties, it is essential for leaders to cultivate self-awareness and address the roots of their internal resistance. By recognizing and challenging our self-limiting beliefs, we can begin to build self-confidence and develop a more empowering mindset. Seeking support from mentors, coaches, or trusted peers can provide a safe space to explore these challenges and gain insights from others who have experienced similar struggles. Engaging in practices such as self-reflection, mindfulness, and personal development can also help us navigate the complexities of leadership and alleviate the loneliness that arises from internal resistance. Ultimately, by confronting and transforming our internal barriers, we can lead with greater authenticity, resilience, and effectiveness.

THE LONELINESS OF LEADING TOXIC PEOPLE

Leading toxic individuals can be an intricate and demanding endeavor for any leader. This chapter aims to provide a comprehensive understanding of the challenges and complexities associated with navigating the dynamics of toxic relationships. In this chapter, we will delve into the unique characteristics and behaviors exhibited by toxic individuals, shedding light on their manipulative tactics, disruptive influence, and detrimental effects on team dynamics. Through real-life examples and relatable scenarios, we will paint a vivid picture of the challenges faced by leaders in dealing with toxic people.

The presence of toxic individuals can have a profound impact on leaders' overall well-being and effectiveness. In this section, we will explore the various ways in which toxic individuals can erode a leader's confidence, create emotional turmoil, and undermine their decision-making capabilities. By delving into the emotional toll and psychological strain that toxic relationships impose, we will shed light on the potential consequences, such as burnout, stress, and compromised mental health. Moreover, we will emphasize the importance of recognizing these impacts and taking proactive measures to safeguard the leader's well-being, resilience, and ability to lead effectively in the face of toxicity.

The definition and manifestations of toxic behavior in different contexts can vary, but at its core, toxic behavior refers to patterns of conduct that are harmful, disruptive, and detrimental to individuals and their surrounding environment. In this section, we will explore the multifaceted nature of toxic behavior and how it can manifest in various contexts, such as workplaces, relationships, and social settings.

Toxic behavior can take many forms, including but not limited to manipulation, deceit, bullying, intimidation, and emotional abuse. We will delve into these manifestations and provide real-life examples to illustrate the detrimental impact they have on individuals and their interactions. By examining toxic behavior in diverse contexts, we will highlight the common threads that tie them together, emphasizing the need for leaders to be vigilant and adept at identifying toxic dynamics.

Understanding the underlying causes and motivations of toxic behavior is crucial for effectively addressing and mitigating its impact. We will delve into the root causes that may contribute to toxic behavior, such as deep-seated insecurities, unresolved traumas, power imbalances, and a lack of emotional intelligence. It may be possible to source the root of the issue as a leader, but be careful not to get sucked into their manipulative behavior. Toxic people are often master manipulators. So as good of a leader as you may be, they are often more skilled at manipulating.

By gaining a clear understanding of the definition, manifestations, and underlying causes of toxic behavior, leaders can develop a nuanced approach to dealing with toxic individuals. You can employ strategies to mitigate the impact of toxic behavior, promote healthier dynamics, and encourage a supportive and respectful environment for all. Through education and awareness, leaders can cultivate a culture that rejects toxic behavior and encourages personal growth, emotional well-being, and positive collaboration.

To me, this seems like a good place to put in a caveat: in today's self-diagnosis culture where everyone is a psychologist because they have gone to therapy or follow a therapist on social media, many people have gone really overboard with what toxicity is in a person. I do believe that countless people have benefitted from the openness of diagnosis and symptoms, but good mental health professionals have studied and gained great skills to understand far better than those who aren't trained can. Just because you don't like someone, or don't like how someone spoke to or treated you doesn't mean that they are toxic. Furthermore, there is a gross overuse of the term "gaslighting." With what I feel is a dramatic increase in narcissistic behavior, it stands to reason the term is more applicable but gaslighting is a very specific term with a specific meaning.

A few years ago there was a sensational argument on the internet about a dress, whether it was gold and white or blue and some other color. It was a crazy and useless argument. If you were to have a conversation where someone held one belief and it was contrary to yours, that is not gaslighting.

Let's say you send an email to a coworker with a read receipt attached. You go and see that they have opened it and then they tell you in a meeting that they never received the email and that you must have imagined sending it. That is an example of gaslighting. I want to be clear in this chapter that I am talking about quantifiable toxicity and its effect on leaders.

It is far easier to placate a toxic person rather than confront and deal with all the necessary steps it takes to get them on the right path. The problem is, toxic individuals have a significant impact on organizational culture, often leading to damaging consequences that permeate throughout the entire workplace. Their behavior can erode trust, create an atmosphere of fear and negativity, and hinder collaboration and productivity.

One of the primary ways toxic individuals damage organizational culture is by spreading a sense of mistrust and insecurity among team members. Their manipulative tactics, deceitful practices, and tendency to play favorites create an environment where employees are constantly on guard and reluctant to collaborate openly. This breakdown in trust hampers communication, stifles creativity, and erodes morale, ultimately impeding the overall performance of the organization.

Moreover, toxic individuals often exhibit aggressive and bullying behaviors, which can create a hostile work environment. They belittle and demean others, engage in power struggles, and use their influence to intimidate and control those around them. Such behavior not only creates an atmosphere of fear and discomfort but also inhibits innovation and stifles the free exchange of ideas. Employees become hesitant to take risks or voice their opinions, leading to a culture of silence and conformity that stifles growth and progress.

Additionally, toxic individuals can spread negativity like wildfire within an organization. Their constant criticism, gossip, and pessimism create a toxic atmosphere that permeates every interaction and decision-making process. This negativity becomes contagious, affecting the attitudes and behaviors of other team members, leading to a downward spiral of low morale and diminished motivation. It becomes increasingly challenging to maintain a positive and inclusive culture when toxic behavior goes unchecked.

The damage inflicted by toxic individuals on organizational culture can be long-lasting and far-reaching. It takes a toll on employee well-being, engagement, and satisfaction, resulting in higher turnover rates and decreased productivity. Leaders must be proactive in addressing toxic behavior and fostering a culture of respect, open communication, and accountability. By promoting healthy relationships, setting clear expectations, and swiftly addressing toxic behavior, leaders can mitigate the damage and create a more positive and thriving organizational culture.

Toxic individuals have a profound ability to cause isolation and loneliness among leaders, creating an overwhelming sense of detachment and disconnection. N Their toxic behaviors, such as manipulation, backstabbing, and spreading rumors, create a hostile environment where leaders feel isolated and cut off from their colleagues and support networks. In this section, we will explore how toxic people contribute to the isolation and loneliness experienced by leaders.

One of the ways toxic individuals perpetuate isolation is by actively undermining the relationships and alliances that leaders have worked hard to cultivate. They excel at sowing seeds of discord and creating division among team members, leading to fractured relationships and a breakdown of trust. As a result, leaders find themselves isolated, unable to confide in or rely on their peers, as toxic individuals have eroded the support system they once had. This isolation can be particularly distressing for leaders who previously relied on these relationships for guidance, collaboration, and emotional support.

Toxic people often engage in exclusionary tactics, intentionally marginalizing and isolating leaders from important discussions, decision-making processes, and social events. They manipulate dynamics to ensure that leaders are left out, overlooked, or undermined, making them feel like outsiders within their own teams or organizations. This exclusion breeds feelings of loneliness, as leaders struggle to find a sense of belonging and connection with their colleagues.

Toxic individuals also thrive on creating a toxic work culture where fear and intimidation reign. They undermine the confidence and self-esteem of leaders through constant criticism, gaslighting, and personal attacks. This psychological manipulation can lead to a sense of isolation, as leaders start to question their own worth and abilities. The constant negativity and hostility chip away at their emotional well-being, making them feel isolated and lonely in their leadership roles.

The isolation and loneliness caused by toxic individuals have severe consequences for leaders' mental health and overall well-being. It can lead to increased stress, burnout, and a diminished sense of purpose. Leaders may begin to doubt their capabilities and question their decisions, further exacerbating feelings of isolation and loneliness. It becomes crucial for leaders to recognize their toxic behaviors, set boundaries, and seek support from trusted allies and mentors who can provide guidance, empathy, and a sense of connection.

In combating the isolation and loneliness caused by toxic individuals, leaders must prioritize self-care and personal growth. They can seek out like-minded individuals who share their values and aspirations, fostering genuine connections and relationships. Building a strong support network outside of the toxic environment can provide a sense of camaraderie and validation. Additionally, leaders should focus on their own personal development, honing their leadership skills and cultivating resilience to navigate challenging situations with toxic individuals.

By acknowledging the impact of toxic people on their isolation and loneliness, leaders can take steps to break free from the toxic dynamics, cultivate healthy relationships, and create a more supportive and inclusive work environment. It is crucial for leaders to prioritize their well-being, seek professional guidance if necessary, and surround themselves with positive influences that uplift and inspire them.

I was meeting with a man who ran an Alcoholics Anonymous type of group within the church. He was very proficient and knowledgeable in addiction having spent a great deal of time studying the topic up close and personal within his own family and vocationally. He told me a story where a woman had come to the meeting as the mother of an adult son who was an alcoholic. She shared that her son who was an alcoholic for around 20 years would outwit her every time she tried to confront him about his drinking. She would always leave feeling like she was in the wrong.

It was after she met with the pastor she understood that the son's brain was pickled and he was definitely not smarter than she was. Also, she was not wrong for wanting a better life for him. However, he was so experienced in his manipulation, he would make her feel like she was a wicked and evil mom. This was the painful point she had; she already questioned her performance as a mother since she raised someone who became an alcoholic. This is something that skilled manipulators do, they are keenly aware of things that are sensitive areas within your life and they exploit it when you try to confront their performance or behavior.

As leaders, it is essential to establish clear boundaries and enforce appropriate consequences when dealing with toxic individuals. First and foremost, leaders must define their boundaries and communicate them effectively. This involves articulating what behaviors are unacceptable and explicitly conveying expectations for respectful and constructive interactions. By setting clear boundaries, leaders create a framework that guides their interactions with toxic individuals and helps protect their own well-being and the well-being of their team.

Once boundaries are established, it is crucial to enforce consequences when those boundaries are violated. Consequences send a powerful message that toxic behaviors will not be tolerated and that there are repercussions for their actions. The consequences should be appropriate and proportionate, aligning with the severity and frequency of the toxic behavior. This can range from verbal warnings, written documentation, and reassignment of responsibilities, to formal disciplinary actions, depending on the organization's policies and the specific circumstances.

However, it is essential to approach consequences with a fair and objective mindset. Leaders should gather evidence and documentation of toxic behaviors, ensuring a factual basis for implementing consequences. Emotions should be set aside, and decisions should be made impartially, focusing on the impact of the toxic behavior on individuals and the organization as a whole.

Additionally, leaders should foster a culture that encourages open communication and reporting of toxic behavior. It is essential to provide a safe space for team members to voice their concerns and report incidents without fear of retaliation. Leaders should actively listen to these concerns and take appropriate action, demonstrating their commitment to addressing toxic behaviors and promoting a healthy work environment.

Furthermore, leaders should lead by example and model the behavior they expect from others. By demonstrating respect, empathy, and professionalism, leaders set the tone for acceptable conduct within the team. This can help create an environment where toxic behaviors are less likely to thrive and where individuals feel supported and valued.

By establishing boundaries and implementing appropriate consequences, leaders create a framework for managing toxic behaviors in a constructive and proactive manner. This approach helps protect the well-being of both the leader and the team while promoting a positive work environment where individuals can thrive. Through consistent enforcement and modeling of desired behaviors, leaders can cultivate a culture of respect, collaboration, and productivity, free from the detrimental effects of toxic individuals.

The ultimate "win" if you will in dealing with toxic individuals is to actually help them change their behavior. For that, leaders can employ various tools and tactics to support them in changing their behavior and contributing to a healthier work environment.

1. Constructive Feedback: Leaders should provide timely and

specific feedback to toxic individuals, focusing on their behaviors rather than personal attacks. By highlighting the negative impact of their actions and offering suggestions for improvement, leaders can encourage self-reflection and create opportunities for change.

2. Coaching and Mentorship: Assigning a mentor or coach to work closely with toxic individuals can be an effective approach. A mentor or coach can provide guidance, support, and accountability, helping them understand the consequences of their behavior and develop alternative ways of interacting with others.

3. Development Opportunities: Offering development opportunities, such as training programs, workshops, or seminars, can assist toxic individuals in gaining self-awareness, empathy, and interpersonal skills. These opportunities provide them with new perspectives and tools for effective communication, conflict resolution, and collaboration.

4. Mediation and Conflict Resolution: In situations where conflicts arise due to toxic behaviors, leaders can facilitate mediation sessions to encourage open dialogue and resolution. Mediation allows all parties involved to express their concerns, understand different viewpoints, and work towards finding common ground.

5. Role Modeling: Leaders should exemplify positive behaviors and create an environment that encourages collaboration and respect. By demonstrating healthy communication, empathy, and accountability, leaders provide a powerful example for toxic individuals to follow and emulate.

6. Encouraging Self-Reflection: Leaders can encourage toxic individuals to engage in self-reflection by asking questions that prompt them to consider the impact of their behavior on others and the overall work environment. This introspection can lead to a deeper understanding of their actions and motivation for

change.

7. Recognition and Reinforcement: When toxic individuals exhibit positive changes in behavior, it is essential to acknowledge and reinforce their progress. Recognition can serve as a motivator and reinforce their commitment to personal growth and maintaining healthier relationships.

8. Support and Resources: Providing access to resources such as counseling services, emotional support, or personal development materials can be beneficial for toxic individuals. These resources can assist them in addressing underlying issues or developing coping mechanisms to manage their behavior effectively.

It is important for leaders to approach these tools and tactics with patience, empathy, and a genuine belief in the potential for change. While not all toxic individuals may respond positively or be willing to change, providing them with opportunities and support increases the likelihood of transformation. Leaders must also balance their efforts to support toxic individuals with protecting the well-being and morale of the overall team.

By employing these tools and tactics, leaders can help toxic individuals recognize the need for change, empower them with resources and support, and facilitate their growth and development. Ultimately, the goal is to create an environment where toxic behaviors are replaced with healthier and more constructive interactions, fostering a positive and productive work culture for everyone involved.

Recently I was teaching about the people we meet on the street, random people in our lives whom we have little or momentary interactions with. I was showing pictures of Japanese watermelons that are grown in the shape of cubes or hearts. Oranges in the shape of stars, or even a pear in the shape of Buddha. These fruits are shaped by their environment, and so are we all shaped by our experiences and environment. I have seen many people excel and grow when they are in a healthy environment. So, equally important to the protection of your safe and healthy work environment is, helping the toxic people to be influenced by the new environment.

WHAT DO I DO ABOUT LONELINESS? MY OWN HABITS

In the fast-paced and demanding world of leadership, it's all too easy to prioritize the needs of others while neglecting our own well-being. However, self-care is not just a luxury or a fleeting indulgence—it is an essential practice for leaders to maintain their physical, mental, and emotional health. In this chapter on ways to practically deal with loneliness, we delve into the significance of prioritizing self-care as a leader and explore the transformative effects it can have on both personal and professional realms. From nurturing physical vitality to fostering emotional resilience, this chapter offers practical insights and actionable strategies to help leaders cultivate a sustainable and holistic self-care routine. By investing in our own well-being, we not only enhance our effectiveness as leaders but also model a healthy and balanced approach to those we lead.

Before you cut to the next chapter, I want to say that we will be breaking some of the misconceptions about the term "Self-Care." We will be discussing what are some ways that someone can truly care for themselves. You being your most healthy optimum self is how you will attract healthy people into your life, be able to put guards up between you and those that are unhealthy, and just continue the road that you are on.

Regardless of your religious background, there is measurable truth to the idea of attraction. The actual process or how it works can be debated. But purely from a psychological and manifestation perspective, we know that our subconscious doesn't like to be wrong, so when we say things about ourselves, our subconscious goes to work to prove ourselves right. There are also various studies that correlate likeness to be in relationship with each other. Homophily is a fascinating phenomenon that sheds light on how individuals form social connections with others who share similar characteristics, interests, values, or backgrounds. It manifests in various aspects of life, including friendships, romantic relationships, and professional networks. Countless studies have delved into the role of homophily in social relationships, revealing intriguing patterns and insights.

Research has consistently shown that people have a natural inclination to form friendships with those who possess similar demographic characteristics. For instance, individuals are more likely to forge connections with others who are of similar age, gender, or ethnicity. This tendency can be attributed to the sense of familiarity and shared experiences that arise from these commonalities. Additionally, individuals are drawn to those who hold similar attitudes, beliefs, and values, as these shared perspectives create a sense of cohesion and facilitate smooth interactions.

One notable study published in the Proceedings of the National Academy of Sciences explored the influence of homophily in online social networks. By examining social networking sites, the researchers discovered that individuals tend to connect with others who have comparable interests, educational backgrounds, and geographic locations. This finding highlights how homophily shapes the formation of virtual communities or "echo chambers" where individuals are exposed to information and opinions that align with their existing beliefs and values. Such reinforcing interactions within these echo chambers can influence the development and reinforcement of individual perspectives.

So, while it's very important to actively and intentionally seek out people with differing opinions and ideas, we will inherently attract people who are similar to us. Again, lonely, sad, and unhealthy? Vibrant, energized, and fresh? One of the ways we can break free is by making sure we are healthy.

Starting with the idea of "Self-care." Many people, especially very young professionals have taken the term and made it into some sort of eat-pray-love, thing where people just say, whatever they want, to whoever they want, whenever they want. Or they say, I worked for a whole hour and need to take a self-care break. It may seem harsh, but I have had multiple clients come to me to try to decipher the code of how to work with the younger generation. They would come to me with genuinely positive motives, hoping to understand and support the younger generation of professionals coming into their company. The fact is, there are some amazing young people who have a lot of grit and a strong work ethic. But there are also a lot of young people who have been fooled by social media into thinking everyone can be an influencer and make money taking pictures of themselves at spa facilities in Bali calling it "Self-care" There are many people who do make money doing this. There are many deceived young people who don't know that much of social media is fake, and those who are making money actually are serious hustlers.

True self-care is simply taking care of yourself. It is the same idea as securing your own oxygen mask before you help those around you. There will be seasons of imbalance, but if it becomes a constant state for you then there is a greater underlying problem that needs to be dealt with.

Do you take any days off? I used to wear my 80-hour work week like a badge of honor. The problem was I became very unpleasant to work with and no longer did my job effectively. I used to think that I was just such a dedicated employee or business owner, but the truth is, I was so worried that I wasn't really doing my job well so if I could distract those around me by how "hard" I was working they wouldn't notice. What is actually important? That I do my job well or do I look like I am doing my job well? There is an old story that was most recently told by a great leader named Simon Sinek where he said, two men went out into the woods every day to cut wood. Every day one of the men would disappear for an hour and a half. At the end of the day, they would both have the same amount of wood cut. One day the man who stayed asked the man who left, "Every day you leave and every day you still cut as much as I do, how is that possible and where in the world are you going?" The man who leaves says, "Oh, I go home and sharpen my axe and eat lunch."

See, it is so easy to think that the only way to get someplace is to keep going and keep going. However, that is often not the case. Here are a few ways that we are affected by appropriate rest:

1. Improved cognitive performance: Adequate rest, particularly quality sleep, enhances cognitive functioning, memory consolidation, and learning. Research shows that well-rested individuals demonstrate improved attention, problem-solving abilities, creativity, and decision-making skills compared to those who are sleep-deprived or fatigued.

2. Enhanced productivity and work performance: Rest is not just about taking breaks but also about incorporating periods of recovery and rejuvenation into daily routines. Studies have found that regular breaks and periods of rest throughout the workday can improve productivity, job satisfaction, and overall work performance. Strategic breaks, such as short walks, mindfulness exercises, or engaging in enjoyable activities, can restore focus, reduce stress, and boost energy levels.

3. Physical health and well-being: Appropriate rest is essential for maintaining physical health and well-being. Research has shown that insufficient or poor-quality sleep can contribute to various health issues, including an

increased risk of chronic conditions such as cardiovascular disease, obesity, diabetes, and compromised immune function. Conversely, prioritizing restful activities, engaging in regular exercise, and adopting relaxation techniques can promote physical health, reduce stress levels, and improve overall well-being.

4. Mental and emotional well-being: Rest plays a vital role in supporting mental and emotional well-being. It helps regulate mood, reduce stress, and enhance resilience. Studies have found that individuals who engage in regular relaxation practices, mindfulness, and leisure activities experience lower levels of anxiety, depression, and burnout. Restorative activities, such as hobbies, socializing, and spending time in nature, can contribute to a greater sense of happiness, fulfillment, and life satisfaction.

5. Long-term success and longevity: Prioritizing appropriate rest is associated with long-term success and longevity. Research has demonstrated that individuals who maintain a healthy work-life balance, engage in self-care practices, and consistently practice good sleep hygiene are more likely to achieve sustainable success in their personal and professional lives. Rest allows for rejuvenation, prevents burnout, and promotes sustained performance and achievement over time.

Everyone will find their energy in different things. Some people will be energized by things that drain others. Figuring out what you need and how much you need of it is a crucial need to sustain yourself as a leader. Also, allowing others to be different from you is something that is also needed to be able to lead and work with others.

There is a book that I highly recommend called The 6 Types of Working Genius. The premise is quite simple but equally profound. Patrick Lencioni says there are 6 types of personality traits he calls working genius. They are broken into 3 categories, they are Ideation, Activation and, Implementation. Within the three categories, there are two genius'. In Ideation, it's Wonder and Invention, in the Activation category it is Discernment and Galvanizing. Finally, in Implementation, the two types are Enablement and Tenacity.

The theory so far I have personally found to be accurate among clients as well as the thousands of people researched. It says that every person has two genius, 2 competencies, and 2 frustrations. So when you are working within your genius you can actually be energized from your work. Your competencies are roles within your work that often you have been forced to perform so you have developed a level of competency but it doesn't really energize you to work within these genius'. Frustrations are things that drain you when you are stuck having to work within these roles. I recommend taking the simple online assessment, it should take you about 10 minutes and will help you narrow down the areas of work that you want to try to avoid as best as possible as well as areas that you should focus on. This is a prime example of the need to be a true entrepreneur. Find those people who derive life from doing the things that will crush you over time. YOU DON'T HAVE TO DO IT ALL! In fact, as you discover what your professional frustrations are, you'll be able to ask your team if any of them have a genius in that area. This is one of the most powerful ways you can revamp your team almost immediately.

Okay, now take a deep breath because the next thing I am going to recommend is… meditation. I am not one who thinks too much about spiritually driven meditation even though I am generally very focused on spiritual things. When I teach a class on meditation I will mention the spiritual aspect of it once or twice up front. From there it is all about the measured medical benefits to include the psychological impact as well as physiological.

Science has concluded that our bodies are here in the now. I believe that our souls are not bound to a temporal anchor. Our minds are almost always worrying about the future or thinking about the past. It is a skill that must be practiced for a person to be able to be in the same place at the same time. Meditation and being mindful is the only practice that I have experienced that will help you get there.

For me, meditation is not about chanting or praying, or doing anything that one might consider weird. Meditation as I teach is rather when you pay attention to your breathing and breath in a specific rhythmic pattern. It can be explained in about two sentences: Breathe in for 3 seconds, hold that breath for 3 seconds, then breathe out for 5 seconds. If thoughts come into your mind, just let them come and go, similar to cars driving outside your office building. They come and go all day long but you don't take the time to check out each one and think about the details of those cars.

I recommend that you find a quiet place where you can be alone for five minutes. Do this exercise two or three times per day to start. The profound impact it will have will usually surprise you if you don't already do this. If you can't spare ten minutes out of your day then I would refer you back to the story of the two lumberjacks. It will always be worth the moment that you will take to collect yourself. This breathing exercise is one that never fails to amaze me. On one hand, I have seen it work without fail with every client I have invited to try it. However, it always blows my mind the testimonies that they come back to share about how much it changed their whole world throughout the day after a few days to a week of breathing daily.

Exercise. For some, this is such an evil word. I won't bother getting into the studies that have been done about the effects on mental health that come from exercise because it's so well documented. I will say that for you leader, it cannot be ignored, forgotten, or skipped. The need for you to be in the gym or however you exercise is more than fundamental for you.

Exercise doesn't need to come in the form of going to the gym.

Maybe that's what it is for you, but find the thing that will get your blood flowing and your muscles working. No disrespect to my golfers out there, whereas playing golf is better than nothing, a Harvard Medical article says that you need to add something additional a couple of days per week. Also, the golf exercise only comes from walking between holes so if you are going on a golf cart it's not quite the same. The great news though, is as you go to the gym or exercise in your way, if you are doing it right, you will also improve your golf game!

Exercise is one of the best ways to lower the risk of heart problems. It is twofold, the actual act of exercising your heart will help to make you stronger. Second, since stress is one of the major contributors in terms of heart problems among high-level leaders, exercise is known to reduce stress as well. So there is truly no reason not to get on the tennis court or the track or the pool or whatever! One key point I want to make is, Get over yourself! It is extremely uncomfortable sometimes to get to the gym or start working out because as leaders there may be the concern that you will encounter someone who you lead. The fear of looking ill-prepared or weak, because you can't run as long or lift as much weight, is very real. However, it's also unnecessary and truly unhelpful. You need to make the decision for yourself that you are going to do what is necessary to get better, to be healthy, and to create the pathway for being able to do your job well and for as many years as possible.

I do want to say that I am speaking from personal experience. Since I left my athletic life after college, I have struggled with my weight which has caused me to feel less motivated to exercise. Also, because I grew up doing very regular physical activities, I never developed any type of discipline when it comes to exercise. I used to go on crash diets because I had a big speaking engagement or something to attend where I wanted to look better. Unfortunately, not only was that highly unhealthy, but it also never worked. I have since made the life decision that I will take however many months or years it takes to get to a place of physical health. I can't describe the impact it has had on my mental health as well. The issues that seemed insurmountable, have all become within reach. However, to break out of this cycle of allowing work to consume me and absorb the time I would have normally gone to work out, I enlisted the help of a couple of friends who were in a similar boat and motivated to change.

Furthermore, the last time I made a genuine attempt at getting to the gym, I was younger and cared much more about what others thought. So much so that one time I made this big plan to make all the physical changes at once, I hurt myself pretty seriously pushing far past my limits at that time. By the time I recovered, I was so deflated that I didn't want to go back to the gym, and I also was a little nervous to go back and hurt myself again.

This time though, after realizing the number of times I have offended people, disappointed them made them angry, or whatever mistake I made as a leader, I don't care nearly as much anymore. For example, I used to look at a weight rack and see that someone was lifting more than me. I would think back to the days in high school when I had a weight trainer who had a Ph.D. in weight lifting. I could lift a lot, maybe even more than what that person was lifting. Younger, insecure Danny with something to prove would have walked up and said, "I have done it before, I must be stronger than that guy." Then boom – No gym for at least 6 weeks. Nowadays, I have experienced enough life to know that just like in my professional life, I didn't wake up an experienced executive coach and leader. I went through years and years of mistakes, classes, mentorship, and other things to get to where I am. The same has happened to me in my physical health. I am a good executive coach, if you had told me I would be where I am 17 years ago when I began the journey, I would have arrogantly said, "Of course!" but in the first few years, I would learn that leading people comes with great heartache and even more mistakes. But with one small step after another, one apology for making a mistake that caused offense or a project to have problems after another I would find my way to where I am today. I am still growing and will continue to do so until my last breath on earth.

I now walk into the gym and see these younger guys lifting lots of weight or doing cool pull-ups that I still struggle with, with eyes of aspiration rather than frustration. I have tried to adopt the mindset, when I see someone who is stronger than I am, if it's a particular exercise I want to get better at, I think to myself, "Wow that guy is so strong and I want to be able to do that one day." On the other hand, I once saw this guy kicking the heavy bag and it was so hard it was shaking the floor a bit underneath. This isn't an exercise that I want to be that good at, so I just think to myself, "Man that's cool, that guy is going to pull a Capitan America and send that bag flying!" As opposed to the attitude of, "Yeah I could do that 'cause I am so tough."

Here's the thing; I apply that to my professional life now as well. When I was a young leader, I would compare myself to others, and do what I could to be better than them. There is nothing wrong with wanting to be the best at things but it's the mentality that is off. On one hand, it's like a young guy trying to prove to someone else who is currently better at something, "I'm the man!" On the other hand, it is, "I see how great that person is at this thing, and I want to set my goal to outperform him or her one day." As I mentioned, "If it's an exercise that I want to grow in." So as such, I have no desire to grow too much in my accounting ability. I can do it, but I dislike it so much I am happy to see how amazing someone else is at it and leave it to them.

When I adjusted my mindset to be more open to others succeeding, I no longer need to prove anything, I just need to make sure everyone gets to the same place in the end – the island of success, however, you are measuring it. I have realized that one of the greatest blocks to intimacy or healthy relationships is ego. I have heard leaders say things like, "If people knew how I really felt about myself they wouldn't follow me." So they put up a front that they have it all together and are the best at what they do, unwilling to ask for or receive help. Or I have had people tell me that they learned from leaders they served under that the only way to maintain your respect was to be distant and cold, again to hide the potential that you may not be able to "lift as much weight" as someone who is supposed to be your subordinate.

One of the key factors to this journey is something that I ask all my clients when we get to the topic of longevity and self-care. What does your diet look like? I know, no one wants to be told that the one thing that is readily available that will give you a small shot of dopamine is something you should probably avoid but, it's likely true. Specifically referring to unhealthy foods that are high in sugar. In my experience, the majority of the leaders I talk to say they are too busy to eat healthy. The harsh reality is, they are not too busy to do so, they just don't prioritize eating healthy. I am not here to judge or condemn you for your eating habits. I only changed when it got so bad, I was genuinely scared about my physical future. So I have no judgment for others.

I am not a dietitian, and I don't know what is best for your body. I do recommend if you are able, having a meeting with one and figuring out where you are in your eating habits. The things in our food today dramatically impact our mental and physical health to a concerning level. Another issue that leaders have with their diet, is eating whatever, whenever. Find ways to plan things out, or if you have an assistant or someone who can help, try not to let hunger just happen. Don't forget to eat.

Hobbies, if you can find a hobby that is productive and healthy it can drastically improve your emotional and mental health. If you can find a hobby that helps keep you physically active, this can be a way to get exercise without having to go to the gym since I know many people don't enjoy it. I have enjoyed many different hobbies, perhaps a few more than normal based on my struggles with ADHD, but nevertheless, I have found great enjoyment in these activities. Find something that brings excitement and a little spark of fun to your week.

This next part may sound like a personal promotion but it's true. Find a coach! It doesn't have to be me but find a top-tier executive coach. We serve in countless roles when it comes to supporting professionals. One of the highest functions we serve is as a confidential advisor. All professional executive coaches adhere to a strict confidentiality policy, in fact as a coach, I will not disclose anything to the sponsor without written consent from the coachee. Meaning that even if a manager hires me to coach a subordinate, we will set the terms that I will disclose the attendance of the coachee, and usually that is all. Any further disclosure will be at the express permission of the coachee.

This is such an important factor because there will be things that you as a leader cannot discuss with anyone else safely. Perhaps it is information regarding a business idea that you have and you need to keep it close to the vest before you can even discuss it with your professional team. An executive coach can be someone who gives you feedback on your idea or can simply be a living human who will listen to what you have going on while you process it out loud. Many years ago, actually, before I was an executive coach, I was out having lunch with a pastor friend of mine. I wasn't a staff member nor was I connected to the situation he was processing in any way. However, due to the nature of our relationship and because I have always valued privacy, he was able to share about a situation where he was going to be responsible for firing a pastor based on a moral failure. He was quite devastated, but at the same time, he recognized the severity of the person's poor actions. To be clear these moral issues were not legal moral issues so there was no need to report them, but his actions were clear ground to let him go.

As I sat there, my friend shared how he was very sad about what he needed to do. He was sharing his heartbreak that he needed to send someone out of the church, the place where all are welcome. He was processing if there was an alternative compromise but there truly was none. If I were to liken the situation to a corporate scenario. Imagine the CEO finally took a three-week sabbatical after 10+ years with no vacation and the person he left in charge started to spread rumors about the CEO such as cheating on his wife and cooking the books none of which were true and then tried to get the board to vote the CEO out so they could take over. There is no place for this in the corporate world, and there is no place for this in ministry.

Being there for my friend was all he needed to reiterate the situation out loud to understand how unacceptable it is for someone to lie about their boss in order to take over an organization. Especially with the type of lies that he was creating. I was way over my head in that conversation, I was in my early 20s, and as I said, nearly a decade before I would pursue becoming an executive coach. So even being clueless as to what I should say, simply being there was apparently enough for my friend to deal with the situation.

This is just a single example of leadership difficulties that you will face. I imagine that you can think of a couple of circumstances off the top of your head where you were stuck with a painful decision. Did you have someone to discuss it with? If you did, how helpful was it? If not, how do you think things might have been different if you had?

Perhaps there are deeper things going on. Maybe you need to see a counselor or therapist. I recognize that even in the current world, there is still often a strong stigma surrounding going to see a mental health professional but truly there is nothing wrong with getting a little support. I come back to the question, how badly do you want to break free? There is a quote that seems to be credited to multiple people online, "The things that happened to you are not your fault, but you can be sure that it is now your responsibility to deal with them." Sometimes we are dealt a bad hand, and the impact of that hand can be highly difficult to deal with. However, it is still your choice if you want to live with that for the entirety of your life or if you want to walk away from the proverbial chains that your past experiences have on you.

This is also a story where I ended up referring my client to a mental health professional. The story which I have permission to share, but will not be using any names was quite interesting. I will refer to this client as John. John had an issue with a certain employee of his. The employee used to bring their own coffee in to use with the coffee machine. John said that out of the blue, he began to have a strong emotional feeling toward his employee... not a good one. John would go past their desk and start to feel nauseous, anxious, and angry. Turns out, that particular coffee was what a specific teacher growing up used to drink every day.

Back when John was in high school he had a teacher who was just generally awful. The teacher for whatever reason had a problem with John. John shared that he was constantly being blocked from things, as a talented musician he was invited to join a citywide orchestra. However, when it came time to audition, it just happened to be that this teacher was the adjudicator. He ended up in the last chair of the group. This was not good for two reasons, this limited his opportunities for a scholarship which he desperately needed if he were to attend college. Furthermore, when he shared with his parents what happened, his father took the news very hard and used it as another excuse to beat John. John realized his hatred ran deep for this teacher. Since the teacher was no longer alive by the time he had this revelation, he couldn't confront him, and since it was in the past, he couldn't change it.

With appropriate therapy, he was able to reframe it and realize that because he didn't go to college, he ended up in the different roles that he did professionally. As he worked through the field he was in, he saw a massive need and decided he would find a way to fill it. His grit came from the fact that he was unrelenting in his drive to succeed. Was it a terrible ordeal he went through? Absolutely! Was it fair or his fault? No not in the slightest. However, through it all, he was able to succeed and he didn't even realize that he was using this hardship as motivation. Once he was able to make peace with the past, he was no longer controlled by what happened. He was able to kindly, and without the rage he was feeling previously ask the employee if there was a significance to the particular coffee that he would drink. He said it was his favorite after searching for a long time. John understood and realized as he smelled the coffee in that moment that his affinity for his employee now vastly overshadowed his triggers from the past and he didn't discuss the coffee situation any further.

We all go through things. Some are more severe than others, and things affect us all differently. Take a look at your life and reactions to things, and ask those who are closest to you if they think you need some sort of support.

WHAT DO I DO ABOUT LONELINESS? THE ENVIRONMENT AROUND YOU

This chapter is more of a continuation of the previous chapter than anything else. We are going to focus on specific things that you can do that are a little more external than just you taking care of yourself.

First I want to talk about your support network. There are two types of networks that I would like to discuss. The first one is your professional network and the second one is what I call your "Life-team." I didn't come up with the term Life-team it was a term I learned from Dr. John Townsend. I want to break down the two different teams, their purpose, and their significance.

Your professional network or team, these people in your life are usually in a similar field, or within your company. These people know about the work that you do and understand the work itself or at least are able to support you professionally. For example, maybe you are in advertising but there is someone in your professional network that may not know about advertising but they do understand how to run a successful company. These are people you bring your professional struggles to, especially if you are looking for feedback specific to technical issues or questions that you may be facing. Here is a list of some traits that I would look for in your professional support network:

1. Trustworthy: Look for individuals who are reliable, honest, and maintain confidentiality. Trust is essential for open and meaningful conversations.

2. Empathetic: Seek out individuals who demonstrate empathy and understanding. They should be able to listen attentively, show compassion, and provide support when needed.

3. Positive Attitude: Look for people who have a positive outlook and can provide encouragement and motivation. They should uplift you during challenging times and inspire you to grow.

4. Good Communication Skills: Effective communication is crucial in a support network. Seek individuals who can articulate their thoughts clearly, actively listen, and offer constructive feedback.

5. Knowledgeable and Experienced: Look for individuals who have relevant expertise or experience in areas that align with your goals. They can provide valuable insights, guidance, and mentorship.

6. Open-Minded: It's beneficial to have people in your support network who are open to diverse perspectives and ideas. They should be willing to challenge your thinking and offer alternative viewpoints.

7. Growth-Oriented: Seek individuals who are committed to personal and professional growth. They should be proactive learners, willing to share their knowledge and help you develop new skills.

8. Reliability: Look for people who follow through on commitments and are dependable. They should be responsive and available when you need support or advice.

9. Resilient: Having individuals in your network who have overcome challenges and demonstrated resilience can provide inspiration and guidance during difficult times.

10. Authenticity: Seek individuals who are genuine and authentic. They should be comfortable being themselves and encourage you to do the same.

Remember, building a support network is a personal process, and it's important to find individuals who align with your values, goals, and aspirations.

Here are some steps that could help you find such people:

1. Identify your needs and goals: Determine the specific areas you could benefit from support. It could be in areas such as leadership development, and industry knowledge. Clarify your goals and objectives to guide your networking efforts.

2. Seek out mentors: Look for experienced professionals who can provide guidance, advice, and support. Mentors can offer insights based on their own experiences and help you navigate challenges. Reach out to potential mentors within your organization, industry associations, or professional networks.

3. Join professional associations and networks: Partake in industry-specific associations, networking events, and conferences. These platforms provide opportunities to connect with like-minded professionals, exchange ideas, and gain insights from leaders in your field. Be active and contribute to these communities to build meaningful connections.

4. Attend leadership development programs: Enroll in leadership development programs, workshops, or seminars. These

programs not only enhance your leadership skills but also provide opportunities to network with other leaders. Interacting with peers in a learning environment can develop valuable relationships. It can also help to break up the environment to cause fresh perspectives.

5. Engage in peer groups or mastermind groups: Join or create a peer group or mastermind group where leaders come together to share experiences, challenges, and ideas. These groups offer a confidential and supportive environment to discuss common issues and learn from one another's perspectives.

6. Utilize online platforms and social media: Leverage professional networking platforms like LinkedIn to connect with industry professionals, join relevant groups, and engage in discussions. Engaging in online communities can help you expand your network beyond geographical boundaries.

7. Grow genuine connections: When networking, focus on building authentic relationships rather than merely collecting contacts. Take the time to understand others' needs and offer support where possible. Show genuine interest, actively listen and be willing to contribute to the success of others.

8. Give and receive feedback: Seek feedback from trusted colleagues and mentors to gain valuable insights into your strengths and areas for improvement. Likewise, offer feedback and support to others. Mutual feedback enhances trust and strengthens professional relationships.

9. Maintain and nurture relationships: Building a support network requires ongoing effort. Stay in touch with your connections, offer assistance when needed, and celebrate their successes. Attend networking events regularly and maintain an active online presence.

Remember that building a support network is a reciprocal

process. Be willing to offer support and guidance to others as you seek it for yourself. By nurturing these relationships, you'll create a strong professional support network that can provide guidance, inspiration, and a sense of belonging throughout your leadership journey.

Your Life-team will be similar with some distinct differences; A group of people usually around 8-12 people. They can, and sometimes I believe should be, from different parts of the world if possible. One of the reasons to have people spread out is so that if there is a catastrophe in the middle of the night, you can call someone who is on the other side of the planet when it is the middle of the day for them. These are the people who support you on a more personal level. For me as a Christian, these are people I can call to ask for prayer when I am struggling with something personal. They are people who don't need to have a clue what you do professionally, it can be helpful, but these are more the people who will objectively confront you about decisions you are making from an ethical perspective for every aspect of your life, personally and professionally. Here is a similar list of character traits that I would be looking for in a person I would choose for my Life-team.

1. Trustworthiness: Seek individuals who are trustworthy and dependable. They should respect your confidentiality, maintain their commitments, and be reliable sources of support.

2. Empathy and Compassion: Look for people who show empathy and compassion toward others. They should be able to understand and relate to your emotions and experiences, providing a safe space for you to share and seek advice.

3. Positivity: Surround yourself with individuals who radiate positivity and optimism. They can uplift you during challenging times, offer encouragement, and help you maintain a positive mindset.

4. Active Listening: Choose people who are skilled at active listening. They should be attentive, non-judgmental, and genuinely interested in understanding your thoughts, feelings, and concerns.

5. Non-Critical and Non-Judgmental: Your life team should be composed of individuals who are accepting, non-critical, and non-judgmental. They should create an environment where you feel comfortable being vulnerable and expressing your true self. They also must be willing and able to confront things with honesty and love if they are starting to go off track.

6. Shared Values: Seek individuals who align with your values and beliefs. Shared values can foster deeper connections and understanding, promoting a sense of belonging and mutual support.

7. Diversity: Embrace diversity within your life team. Surround yourself with individuals who come from different backgrounds, cultures, and perspectives. This diversity can offer a broader range of insights and enrich your life experiences. This is part of having people from around the world. Cultural differences can be very helpful in finding innovative solutions to your situation.

8. Growth-Oriented: Look for individuals who are committed to personal growth and development. They should inspire and challenge you to expand your horizons, learn new things, and reach your full potential.

9. Reliability: Choose people who are reliable and consistent in their support. They should be there for you when you need them and follow through on their commitments.

10. Mutual Benefit: Aim for a reciprocal relationship with your life team, where both parties benefit and support each other. It should be a give-and-take dynamic, where everyone contributes to each other's growth and well-being.

In the dynamic and demanding world of leadership, building support networks is of paramount importance. Leaders face unique challenges and responsibilities that can often lead to feelings of isolation and overwhelm. The journey of leadership requires resilience, adaptability, and continuous learning, and having a strong support system can make a significant difference in navigating these challenges effectively.

Leadership is not a solitary endeavor. It involves guiding and influencing others, making tough decisions, and dealing with the pressures of high expectations. The weight of these responsibilities can be overwhelming at times, and leaders may find themselves grappling with self-doubt and uncertainty. Building support networks allows leaders to lean on others for guidance, encouragement, and advice. It provides them with a sense of belonging and connection, enabling them to share their experiences and learn from others who have walked a similar path.

By having these networks of people, you will find that someone will probably have the tool you need. From a literal perspective, if you have friends in the construction world and you are also a builder, someone may have the physical tool you need. In a more figurative way, they may have already done something like you are trying to and can give you direction that could potentially save you from a lot of heartache and time. Or maybe they have the tool you need- perhaps it is a different communication methodology that can get through to that one employee who has the potential to be great but you are just having a hard time communicating your expectations to.

Recognizing the importance of support networks is essential for leaders to thrive in their roles. By proactively seeking and nurturing these networks, leaders can strengthen their resilience, enhance their decision-making abilities, and ultimately improve their overall well-being. In the following chapters, we will delve deeper into the value of mentorship, peer networks, and professional communities, providing guidance on how leaders can build meaningful relationships and find the support they need to excel in their leadership journey.

These teams should be picked carefully because they should be the ones who can handle when things go so wrong you need an actual shoulder to cry on. There will be days where you will break down and by having a team that is a safe place for it, you can ensure that your experience will positively impact your company and those in it.

I read many years ago in a marriage book that at some point a wife needs to learn to stop going to her mother and her friends to complain about her husband and learn to talk it out with him directly, in as much as a husband needs to learn to talk things out period. The reason is when a wife continues to complain to her mother or others, they will only hear all the problems about the marriage and this will begin to turn the mother or friend's heart against the husband. Rarely will the same woman go to her mother or girlfriends to say, "Things are better now, he apologized very sincerely and things have changed." Or, "Turns out I was wrong, and I was the problem in the situation." All it does is builds up malice toward the husband. Please know I don't mean to pick on women in this example. It is just traditionally and at the time the marriage book was written that men just keep things to themselves and bottle them up, while women will share their experiences. That said, in the example above, continuing with the wife, it may not be helpful for her to just completely explode and say things that are a little more passionate than she means. Having the opportunity to hash out her feelings, with someone who is level-headed and unbiased can allow for her to figure out what the issue is. Especially in the case of communicating with men, we won't usually just, "Understand or figure it out on our own." Most people regardless of gender are in fact not adept at mindreading to see what it is that you are having an issue with. And furthermore, many people really want to be reasonably compromising, but if they don't understand your needs then it won't happen. If you can't articulate your needs then they won't know them or be able to make adjustments either.

Similarly, you may have an issue that needs to be discussed and you need a safe place to share your unredacted feelings even if your feelings are not fair or right. They are your feelings so you need to experience and process them. There is clear research that shows when we suppress our feelings it's like throwing a dirty dishrag under the sink, sooner or later that rag will grow into its own problem. However, if you were to wash it a little and then throw it out in the sun to dry it will not continue to grow and will at some point not be an issue at all. If you have the chance to figure out what is really bothering you, first off, when you confront the person, they won't need a hospital or therapist from the excessive verbal beating that you would dole out in your high emotional state. Secondly, if you have fleshed out your issue beforehand, you don't waste time on miscommunication. You can share, when I assigned you _____, I gave you a deadline of _____. It took you 3 extra days and now the consequence is _____, I also feel as though it's personal because it seems that you don't prioritize your job and don't respect the assignment and deadlines I give you, we need to figure this out. As opposed to, "I can't believe you never make deadlines and you are stupid and I just want to fire you."

Yes, I am being a little sarcastic, but I have had leaders who will feel offended by something and so their ability to pinpoint what the employee needs to change gets thrown out the window. Taking the time to process, and taking the time to process with the right people is absolutely imperative for effective leadership.

Many years ago I was told that you should have people below you that you are raising up, people beside you that you can lean on who can also lean on you, and lastly, a mentor or multiple mentors who are raising you up. These people can change throughout your life based on where you are at, and what your role is, but you should always try to be getting poured into, be supported, and pour into others.

One thing that is going to help you in the journey of mitigating the loneliness of leadership is to create a culture around you of honesty and intimacy. I know that many people are afraid of that word, but the fact is you don't really have anything to hide. If you truly do, I would refer you back to getting professional help, dealing with the scary dark things hidden in your closet, and then finding the people you can be honest with once it's been dealt with. Personally, I have found that the people in my circles have zero judgment when I have shared with them the deepest darkest things I have experienced or done in my life. To be clear, I have taken many years to develop my Life-team and my professional team, and I have been careful to curate who is on it. I would highly recommend that you do the same. My team is chosen because if there is a time when I am falling apart and can't handle the decision-making process, I can lean on my team and I know that they will support me with my best as well as my company's best as their first priority.

If you create an environment of honesty and vulnerability, it makes it safe for you as a leader to share. However, your sharing will dramatically impact the culture of safety for your employees or team members as well. As mentioned earlier you want to be three things, a mentor, a mentee, and a team member. The people on your life-team and professional team may be a combination of mentors and accountability/team members because you are not meant to support the people on your team. It may happen that you are also on the life-team of one of your life-team members. For example, on my life-team, only one person on my team has actually asked me to be on their team.

So as discussed earlier in the chapter, finding peer groups can be extremely valuable for you from a survival perspective but can also be incredibly helpful when it comes to growing your business or organization. Professional associations and organizations offer excellent opportunities to connect with peers in your industry or field. These groups often host networking events, conferences, and seminars that facilitate interaction and knowledge-sharing among leaders. By joining these associations, you can gain access to a community of professionals who share similar interests and goals. Actively participate in association activities, contribute to discussions, and seek out opportunities to collaborate with other members. Building genuine relationships within these networks can open doors to mentorship, partnerships, and future opportunities.

Networking events and conferences provide a platform for leaders to expand their network and connect with peers from different organizations or industries. Attend industry-specific conferences, leadership summits, or workshops to meet like-minded individuals who can offer fresh perspectives and insights. Engage in conversations, exchange contact information, and follow up with individuals who resonate with your goals and interests. Participating in panel discussions, giving presentations, or joining panel sessions can also help establish your expertise and credibility within the peer network.

By actively engaging with peer networks, leaders can forge meaningful connections, gain support, and tap into a wealth of knowledge and experiences. These networks provide a fertile ground for collaboration, learning, and professional growth, ultimately enhancing their leadership effectiveness.

Professional communities offer leaders a unique opportunity to connect with like-minded individuals who share a common passion or interest in a particular industry or profession. These communities provide a space for leaders to exchange ideas, share best practices, and collaborate on various initiatives. One of the key benefits of professional communities is access to a diverse range of expertise and perspectives. By engaging with professionals from different backgrounds and experiences, leaders can broaden their knowledge and gain new insights that can enhance their leadership approach. Additionally, professional communities foster a sense of camaraderie and support, creating a network of individuals who understand the challenges and triumphs of leadership.

The next thing that you want to do is find yourself a good or a couple of good mentors. A mentor is someone who has been there. They understand where you are trying to go and they will hopefully save you a few missteps.

Finding the right mentor begins with identifying individuals who possess the knowledge, experience, and qualities that align with your goals and aspirations. Look within your professional network, industry associations, or organizations you are affiliated with to identify potential mentors. Consider leaders who have achieved success in areas you wish to excel in or those whose leadership style resonates with you. Additionally, seek recommendations from colleagues, supervisors, or trusted advisors who can provide insights into potential mentors. It's important to cast a wide net and explore diverse perspectives to find mentors who can offer well-rounded guidance.

Approaching a potential mentor requires a thoughtful and intentional approach. Begin by conducting thorough research about the mentor's background, achievements, and areas of expertise. This will not only demonstrate your genuine interest but also help you tailor your approach when initiating contact. Reach out to the potential mentor through a professional and concise email, expressing your admiration for their work and your desire to learn from them. Highlight specific areas or challenges where you believe their guidance could be invaluable.

When building a relationship with a mentor, it's important to establish clear expectations and boundaries. Clarify the objectives and desired outcomes of the mentorship, ensuring that both parties are aligned on the purpose and scope of the relationship.

Schedule regular meetings or check-ins to discuss progress, seek advice, and address any challenges. Remember that mentorship is a two-way street, so be proactive in seeking feedback, asking thoughtful questions, and showing gratitude for the mentor's time and guidance.

Building trust and rapport with a mentor takes time and effort. Be open and vulnerable about your goals, challenges, and areas where you seek growth. Actively listen to the mentor's insights and perspectives, demonstrating respect for their expertise. Show appreciation for their guidance and acknowledge the value they bring to your development. By investing in the relationship and demonstrating your commitment to learning, you can establish a strong and meaningful connection with your mentor.

Although I truly believe that breathing the same air as someone else, sometimes it just isn't possible. With the advancement of technology, online platforms and communities have become a popular way for leaders to connect and engage with their peers. These virtual communities provide a convenient and accessible space for leaders to interact, share resources, and seek advice from professionals worldwide. Online platforms such as LinkedIn, industry-specific forums, and leadership-focused websites offer a wealth of opportunities to connect with like-minded leaders and join relevant conversations. Leaders can participate in group discussions, contribute to online forums, and follow influential thought leaders to stay updated with the latest trends and developments in their industry. So whereas I do believe in person is always best, sometimes speaking with a brilliant leader making waves on the opposite side of the planet may have to happen online and that's okay.

Finding and engaging with professional communities requires proactive efforts from leaders. Here are some strategies to consider:

1. Research and identify relevant communities: Explore industry-

specific associations, online forums, and professional networks that align with your leadership interests and goals. Conduct research, read reviews, and seek recommendations from trusted colleagues or mentors.

2. Participate actively: Once you've identified relevant professional communities, actively engage by joining discussions, sharing valuable insights, and offering support to fellow members. Actively participate in virtual events, webinars, and workshops organized by these communities.

3. Seek out mentorship opportunities: Many professional communities offer mentorship programs where experienced leaders can provide guidance and support to emerging leaders. Take advantage of these opportunities to connect with mentors who can offer valuable advice and help in your leadership journey.

4. Contribute and share knowledge: Share your expertise and experiences within the community by writing articles, contributing to blogs, or hosting webinars. Sharing your knowledge not only positions you as a thought leader but also raises meaningful connections with other professionals.

By actively seeking and engaging with professional communities, you can expand your network, gain valuable insights, and find support from like-minded individuals. These communities offer a platform for continuous learning, collaboration, and personal growth, enriching the leadership journey of individuals.

Building authentic relationships with colleagues and team members is crucial for leaders to create a sense of connection and support within their professional environment. Authentic relationships are built on trust, open communication, and mutual respect. Leaders can foster these relationships by actively engaging with their team members, showing genuine interest in their well-being, and creating a safe space for open dialogue. By taking the time to understand the strengths, aspirations, and challenges of their team members, leaders can establish a foundation of trust and foster a supportive environment where individuals feel valued and supported.

While on the journey of creating a culture that is open for discussion, try adding team bonding exercises. I would look up what the latest and most effective team bonding is. The reason is, often times the old team building exercises are not well thought of among people who are going through them. They are effective and can help instill the culture you are trying when done right.

Now that we have discussed being a Mentee and a team member, or peer support, let's talk about being a Mentor. I want to encourage you to seek someone out whom you see great potential and begin to speak into their lives. Hopefully, they will take the initiative to ask you to be a mentor to them. Moreover, be willing to mentor someone if they ask you. Never forget what it was like for you starting out. Did you have a mentor? How did that impact you? If you didn't have a mentor what would that have changed if you did?

DEVELOPING LEADERSHIP PRESENCE

Leadership presence is an essential quality that sets exceptional leaders apart from the rest. It encompasses the ability to captivate and inspire others through one's demeanor and communication style. Leadership presence goes beyond mere visibility or authority; it is the intangible essence that commands attention, engenders trust, and influences others to follow.

In the realm of leadership, presence plays a vital role in driving organizational success. It is through a strong and authentic presence that leaders can effectively convey their vision, values, and aspirations, rallying their teams toward a common goal. A leader with a commanding presence is not only seen but also felt, leaving a lasting impression on their followers.

One of the key reasons why leadership presence is crucial lies in its power to inspire and motivate others. When leaders exude confidence, authenticity, and charisma, they create an environment where individuals feel inspired to give their best and go the extra mile. Leadership presence instills a sense of purpose and direction, providing a guiding light for teams to navigate challenges and achieve collective success.

Moreover, leadership presence gives a sense of trust and

credibility. By embodying honesty, integrity, and consistency, leaders build strong relationships with their teams, stakeholders, and peers. When leaders demonstrate authenticity and transparency, they establish a foundation of trust, enabling open communication, collaboration, and innovation.

Leadership presence also extends beyond personal charisma and into the realm of emotional intelligence. Leaders with a strong presence possess the ability to empathize, connect, and understand the needs and concerns of their team members. This empathetic approach creates a sense of psychological safety, where individuals feel valued, heard, and supported. Consequently, it creates an inclusive and collaborative environment that fuels creativity and encourages growth.

Leadership presence is an influential force that shapes the direction and success of organizations. Its significance lies in its capacity to inspire, motivate, and build trust. By cultivating a strong and authentic presence, leaders can create an environment where individuals feel empowered, valued, and confident to contribute their best. Leadership presence sets the stage for collaboration, growth, and the attainment of collective goals, making it a critical attribute for impactful leadership.

Having an open presence as a leader is an indispensable quality that breaks down barriers, invites connection, and eliminates the sense of isolation that can pervade leadership roles. It is an intentional approach that invites others to engage, share, and collaborate, creating a supportive and welcoming environment.

If you have an open presence, it sends a powerful message that you are approachable and receptive to others' perspectives and ideas. It breaks down the walls of hierarchy and establishes a level playing field where individuals feel comfortable voicing their thoughts and concerns. This open presence serves as an antidote to isolation, creating a sense of belonging and camaraderie among team members.

By being open and accessible, leaders create opportunities for meaningful interactions. They actively listen, validate emotions, and encourage open dialogue. This increases trust and psychological safety within the team, as individuals feel confident that their contributions are valued and respected. In turn, this open presence cultivates an environment where collaboration flourishes, ideas are freely shared, and innovation thrives.

Moreover, an open presence as a leader allows for the building of authentic relationships. When leaders are approachable and open, they create opportunities for genuine connections to form. This humanizes the leadership role and breaks down the isolation that can sometimes accompany it. Leaders who have an open presence actively seek to understand their team members, their aspirations, and their challenges. This empathy and understanding contribute to a sense of unity and support, fostering a strong sense of camaraderie and breaking the isolation that leaders may experience.

An open presence also promotes transparency and accountability. When leaders are open in their communication, and sharing information and insights, it creates a culture of transparency within the organization. This openness ensures that everyone is on the same page, reducing misunderstandings and promoting alignment. Furthermore, an open presence encourages leaders to lead by example, taking ownership of their actions and decisions. This accountability promotes trust and strengthens the bond between leaders and their teams.

Having an open presence as a leader is of utmost importance in breaking the isolation often associated with leadership roles. It creates an environment of trust, collaboration, and inclusivity, where individuals feel comfortable expressing themselves and contributing to the collective goals. An open presence advances authentic relationships, transparency, and accountability, paving the way for effective leadership and a thriving organizational culture.

Leadership presence is a multi-dimensional concept that encompasses several key elements, each contributing to a leader's ability to inspire, influence, and connect with others. These elements, when embraced and cultivated, enhance a leader's overall presence and impact.

Confidence is a vital element of leadership presence. It emanates from a deep belief in oneself, capabilities, and the vision being pursued. A confident leader exudes a sense of assurance that instills trust and encourages others to follow. It is an inner strength that enables leaders to navigate challenges, make tough decisions, and inspire others to rise to their full potential. It's important to note, the difference between confidence and arrogance. Confidence is simply knowing full well what you can and can't do and being willing to put your best foot forward. Arrogance is what happens when you are not sure of yourself and you put up an inauthentic front in order to get people to think you can.

Authenticity is another crucial aspect of leadership presence. Authentic leaders are genuine, transparent, and true to themselves. They bring their whole selves to their leadership roles, embracing their strengths, weaknesses, and vulnerabilities. By being authentic, leaders create a genuine connection with their teams, enhancing trust and creating a safe space for open communication and collaboration.

Effective communication plays a pivotal role in leadership presence. It involves not only the ability to articulate ideas clearly but also active listening and empathetic understanding. Leaders who communicate effectively engage in meaningful dialogue, ensuring that messages are understood, concerns are addressed, and ideas are heard. Through compelling communication, leaders inspire, motivate, and align their teams toward shared goals.

Charisma is an element that amplifies leadership presence. It is an innate quality that draws people in, captivating and inspiring them. Charismatic leaders possess a magnetic energy that influences and motivates others to follow their lead. This element of leadership presence is characterized by passion, enthusiasm, and the ability to create a compelling vision that resonates with others.

Finally, emotional intelligence is a critical element of leadership presence. Leaders with high emotional intelligence understand and manage their own emotions while empathetically connecting with the emotions of others. This enables them to navigate interpersonal dynamics, resolve conflicts, and build strong relationships based on trust and respect. Emotional intelligence allows leaders to create an inclusive and supportive environment, fostering collaboration and unleashing the full potential of their teams.

Leadership presence encompasses key elements such as confidence, authenticity, effective communication, charisma, and emotional intelligence. By cultivating these elements, leaders enhance their ability to make a lasting impact, inspire others, and create meaningful connections. Leadership presence is a dynamic and evolving quality that, when nurtured, enables leaders to lead with influence and authenticity.

Becoming self-aware and understanding the nuances of body language and non-verbal cues is a vital aspect of effective leadership and will directly contribute to presence. It is through this awareness that leaders can better connect with others, have open communication, and build strong relationships.

One key component of self-awareness is recognizing and understanding your own body language. Our body language often communicates messages that words alone cannot convey. By paying attention to our posture, gestures, and facial expressions, we can align our non-verbal signals with our intended messages. Being mindful of how we present ourselves physically allows us to project confidence, openness, and authenticity, making others feel comfortable and engaged in our presence.

As an executive coach, I work to be very aware of what my body is saying. The reason is when I am in a coaching session, although the power dynamic is on an equal level, sometimes coachees perceive a coach as a higher level. One message I am trying to communicate is that we are equal, another is that I am engaged and hearing what they are saying. Finally, I am really wanting to say, "I am not judging you, I am just staying curious about your life." When a coachee is sharing something deeply personal, they are often extra sensitive to what your body is communicating and this can be a big problem if you are communicating judgment.

That said, this may be a big surprise but I am actually very shy if I am in new environments. Although I am a public speaker, I don't like attention being on me as a standard. What I didn't realize is how my body language speaks when I am not paying attention to it. Apparently, I am very unapproachable when I am just trying to be unnoticed. That's not inherently wrong, but as an executive coach who is regularly looking for new clients, I definitely won't meet them in a coffee shop looking as unfriendly as I apparently do. I was made aware of this at church once where it actually is a problem. As a pastor, I definitely shouldn't be so standoffish.

A good friend came up to me and said, "You know Danny, you are one of the most friendly people I know, I mean you are genuinely someone I always enjoy being around." Feeling happy and seeing it as a compliment, I smiled and said, "Aww thanks, I enjoy your company as well." Then my friend looked back at me and said "Yeah... But no one who doesn't know you would ever figure that out from your face."

I was shocked. I guess I always knew that I for lack of a different way of saying it, don't love meeting new people in social settings, but I didn't know that my body was doing whatever possible to make sure that I didn't. Many factors of isolation as a leader are circumstantial or out of our control, however, in my case, some of the loneliness I was experiencing was directly my fault.

Equally important is the ability to interpret the non-verbal cues and vocal tones of others. Leaders who are attuned to these signals can gain valuable insights into the thoughts, emotions, and needs of their team members. By observing subtle changes in body language, such as crossed arms, fidgeting, or eye contact, leaders can detect discomfort or resistance and address it proactively. Additionally, paying attention to vocal tone, pitch, and speed can provide clues about someone's level of confidence, enthusiasm, or engagement. This understanding enables leaders to adjust their approach, offer support, and create a safe and collaborative environment.

I put crossed arms as an example because it is one of the most commonly used examples, however, I also just feel very comfortable with my arms crossed with no underlying emotional reason. It is important to learn finer intricacies but far more importantly is just developing the relationship where you can ask. Don't put emotion behind something if there isn't anything there, but ask the question if you see something. If they say they are fine, and it seems like they mean it, leave it alone until something changes. Don't be afraid to ask in the first place though.

Developing self-awareness and honing the skill of interpreting non-verbal cues and vocal tone requires practice and reflection. Leaders can engage in activities such as mindfulness exercises, role-playing, or working with a coach or mentor to enhance their self-awareness and communication skills. By investing time and effort into developing this aspect of leadership, leaders can grow stronger connections, promote effective collaboration, and create an environment where everyone feels heard and valued.

Personal growth is a lifelong journey that encompasses continuous learning, self-reflection, and intentional development. It is a process of expanding one's knowledge, skills, and perspectives, ultimately leading to greater self-awareness and the ability to make positive changes in various aspects of life. To embark on the path of personal growth, it is essential to embrace curiosity and a growth mindset.

One way to continue personal growth is through reading and seeking knowledge. Engaging with books, articles, and resources relevant to one's interests and areas of growth can provide valuable insights, inspire new ideas, and broaden perspectives. Additionally, attending workshops, seminars, or online courses can offer structured learning opportunities and help acquire new skills or deepen existing ones.

Self-reflection plays a pivotal role in personal growth. Taking time for introspection allows individuals to examine their thoughts, emotions, and behaviors, gaining a deeper understanding of themselves. Journaling, meditation, or engaging in meaningful conversations with trusted individuals can facilitate self-reflection and promote personal growth.

Embracing challenges and stepping out of comfort zones is another powerful way to foster personal growth. By taking on new experiences, pursuing goals that push boundaries, and embracing failure as a stepping stone to learning, individuals can expand their capabilities, build resilience, and develop a sense of confidence and self-assurance.

Cultivating a supportive network of mentors, coaches, and like-minded individuals is instrumental in personal growth. Surrounding oneself with people who inspire, challenge, and encourage growth can provide valuable guidance, feedback, and accountability. Engaging in meaningful conversations, seeking advice, and actively participating in communities or groups with shared interests can create a nurturing environment for personal growth.

Ultimately, personal growth is a continuous journey that requires self-motivation, perseverance, and a commitment to ongoing development. By embracing curiosity, seeking knowledge, practicing self-reflection, embracing challenges, and nurturing a supportive network, individuals can unlock their full potential and experience meaningful personal growth.

Your individual growth should be both professional and personal meaning your skills and your emotions and other issues. Growing up apparently, I experienced a high level of trauma. As is pretty common, I just assumed my experience was normal to everyone else. In my sophomore year in college when I attended straight out of high school, I took a psych class. One day the professor administered some type of trauma survey. After we checked all the boxes that applied we added up the score and a girl in my class said she got a thirty-something, and the whole class gasped. I quietly sat there with a score of somewhere around one hundred and fifty and one hundred and seventy, I don't remember exactly what it was. The bottom line, I was in trouble and didn't even know it.

My early desire to go into psychology was a result of what is known as a wounded healer. I was so broken in my young years that I couldn't support the weight of leadership roles because I would literally crumble under pressure. One day around twenty years old when my world had truly crumbled around me I turned to God and church even though I had never attended a church service in my life. Through my church, I attended many years of ministries that are very effective in healing. In fact, they are so effective they are utilized by prisons, recovery houses, and even adult probation services around the entire country.

Even with more than a decade of working on my healing, there was apparently still work to do. When I attended the Townsend Institute at Concordia in Irvine I was in my mid-30s. Part of the program is that you are required to attend the kick-off conferences in person. While there, you will go through what they call process groups. It's a group where you get the opportunity to bring up something you have experienced and then the group helps you process things. Again, after more than a decade of ministry and professional counseling, I didn't know there was more to be done until I was in the group.

Why in the world would there be a group experience like this for people focusing on business? Simple, if you want to be a leader, you can't be dealing with a broken foundation. As I went through processing some events that took place in my life, I learned that there were things that were still in there that affected how I interacted with the people I was leading. Since then I have continued to figure things out and sharpen my leadership skills. Even though I have pretty much dealt with all the big rocks, I still will attend any healing thing I hear about just because I want to be sure that I am the best version of myself. Especially since I am going to recreate myself in those I lead.

I am not secretive about my past, obviously, as it is here in a book that is being published to the world. However, I am very cautious with whom I will share details and lastly, I only share when I feel it's necessary. My past is just that, past. I am sharing it here as an example of being willing to be transparent in order to help others feel confident in sharing with others as well. There is a great need to be honest and open and yet, you still need to be discerning when, where, and how.

This is something that is especially difficult for pastors, specifically speaking pastors. There is this inherent fear, which I understand, that if they speak up about their struggles, then someone will use it against them. As we talked about early in the book, some leaders are in a position where their personal issues can reduce confidence in the leader of a company damaging the share value. I understand that and, that is all the more reason to find safe people whom you can share things with.

The profound impact that being more open in just my presence is difficult to articulate. After it was pointed out to me that I was seemingly cold and unwelcoming, I decided to be intentionally different. I had people begin to approach me after I made the difference and they would say things like, "I really didn't know you were so friendly." Or, "I was kinda scared to come talk to you before but you're actually really easy to talk to." A little embarrassed by the glaring truth about how I was perceived before, I was also glad that I became aware of it. Now I have developed great relationships with the people at my new church and within my company.

EMBRACING VULNERABILITY

In the world of leadership, vulnerability is often viewed as a sign of weakness or a potential risk to one's authority. However, a growing body of research and experience highlights the profound impact that embracing vulnerability can have on effective leadership. It is a transformative quality that allows leaders to connect with their teams on a deeper level, foster trust and collaboration, and create a supportive environment that encourages growth and innovation. By opening up, sharing their struggles, and being authentic, leaders can build stronger relationships, inspire their teams, and achieve greater success.

Embracing vulnerability in leadership is not without its challenges. Leaders face the pressure to maintain a facade of strength and confidence, fearing that revealing their vulnerabilities may diminish their authority or invite criticism. However, this fear usually contributes to a sense of isolation and a lack of authentic connection with their teams. By shielding themselves from vulnerability, leaders miss out on the opportunity to tap into the true potential of their teams and create an environment where individuals feel safe to take risks, share ideas, and grow professionally.

The impact of avoiding vulnerability in leadership extends

beyond missed opportunities for growth. It perpetuates a culture of fear, stifles creativity and innovation, and hinders the development of meaningful relationships. Leaders who are unwilling to embrace vulnerability may find themselves disconnected from their teams, struggling to motivate and inspire, and facing challenges alone. Therefore, understanding the importance of vulnerability and its impact on leadership is crucial for leaders to unlock their true potential and create an environment conducive to collaboration, growth, and success.

Embracing vulnerability as a leader allows for the breaking down of barriers that often exist between leaders and their teams. When leaders are willing to show their vulnerabilities, whether it's admitting mistakes, seeking help, or sharing personal stories, they create an environment of authenticity and openness. By demonstrating that they are not infallible and that they too face challenges, leaders become relatable and approachable, which paves the way for deeper connections with their team members. This transparency helps to build trust and establishes a foundation of mutual understanding, where individuals feel comfortable sharing their own vulnerabilities and seeking support when needed.

When leaders embrace vulnerability, it sets the tone for a culture of openness and collaboration within the team. By showing vulnerability, leaders invite their team members to do the same, creating an atmosphere where everyone feels comfortable expressing their ideas, concerns, and feedback. This cultivates a sense of psychological safety, where individuals are not afraid of judgment or reprisal and are more likely to contribute their unique perspectives and skills. The result is enhanced collaboration, as team members feel valued and empowered to actively participate in problem-solving, innovation, and decision-making processes. By embracing vulnerability, leaders unlock the full potential of their teams and create an environment that thrives on trust, creativity, and collective success.

Embracing vulnerability as a leader involves being open to learning from failures and embracing feedback. When leaders admit their mistakes and acknowledge areas for improvement, they create a culture that encourages growth and development. By modeling a willingness to learn from failures, leaders demonstrate that setbacks are opportunities for growth rather than sources of shame. This attitude sets a positive example for the entire team, encouraging them to take risks, learn from their own mistakes, and seek feedback to continuously improve. Through this process of embracing vulnerability and learning from failures, leaders and their teams foster a culture of resilience and adaptability, driving personal and professional growth.

We have probably all heard that our children learn from what we do more than what we say. That doesn't change all that much when we are adults. Culture is set based on the behavior of leaders, not on their words. Temporary change can happen when there is a big rah-rah day with a conference or workshop, but lasting change comes when the leader makes the long-term adjustment in their thinking and mindset in order to create new behaviors in themselves. If a leader sets the tone by being honest and open that will communicate that it is safe for others to do the same. By encouraging open communication, leaders create an environment where new ideas can flourish. When team members feel safe to share their thoughts and suggestions, they are more likely to contribute innovative solutions and challenge the status quo. Embracing vulnerability also means being open to experimenting with new approaches and being willing to take calculated risks. This mindset encourages creativity, encourages innovation, and drives the team to explore new possibilities. By creating a culture that values continuous improvement and innovation, leaders cultivate an environment where individuals are empowered to reach their full potential and contribute their unique strengths.

Remember that the largest percentage of the current workforce is the Millennial Generation. While every generation has many, not great qualities they all also have many beneficial qualities. One of the great qualities of the Millennial workforce is their use of the word "Why?" Now this has been a point of great tension, especially between Millennials and Boomers. Boomers were from a generation where you just did what you were told, they were the children of World War 1 and 2 parents. You didn't ask, you just did. However Millennials often didn't accept the status quo, they had to ask, "Why is it like this?" The benefit of a multi-generational workforce is the potential for different traits to be shared with the other generations. If Millennials learned how to just do rather than question a little more that would be a benefit. If Boomers looked a little more at how things are and questioned if there was a better way, there is great potential for a powerful positive impact there as well.

I remember hearing a story when I was young. A woman was making dinner for some friends. She was cooking pasta in a thin frying pan, having to pay very close attention to it so it didn't spill over, adding water as it ran out. One of her friends asked her, "Jess, why are you cooking your pasta in that thin pan?" Her response was, "That's how you cook pasta." The confidence in her answer made the friend take pause. The friend looked around and asked everyone else, "Do you all cook your noodles in a frying pan?" They all looked puzzled and responded, "Of course not, I cook in a pot and just let it cook while I am preparing other dishes."

Jess decided to ask her mom who taught her to cook noodles in a pan why she did it. The mother said, "Well, I guess it's because that's how your grandma taught me." She got the same response from the grandmother when questioned. However, when she called her great-grandmother, she said, "Great-grandma, I've been hearing that you should cook your pasta noodles in a pot, not a pan like you taught us, why does the whole family cook in a pan?" The great-grandmother laughed and said, "Oh sweety, your great-grandfather and I were very poor when we were growing up so when we got married we had nothing. My mother gave me her old frying pan and I cooked everything in that pan. When I finally had a little money, pots were hard to come by because of the war, so we just continued to use the pan for everything."

There was little if any benefit to Jess' cooking method, but it was just, "The way we do things around here." If there was a good reason for it that was beneficial at the end of the "Why do we do this?" Rabbit holes then leave things as they are. However, if there is a better smarter way to do something and no good reason not to change then, make the change. Allowing for these types of questions can be hard. Also, there are times when those questions are just not appropriate and things do just need to be done. But if ever possible, the younger generations that are in the workforce, 40 years and younger, many of them need a reason to do the job and it will alleviate a good amount of stress if you can address the reason up front.

Another thing the millennials began to question is the authenticity of people who were always "Fine" or "good." I have had this discussion with many people, and it actually began with the struggles they were experiencing as low-level leaders working their way up. They would question how all of the older generation is doing so well all the time. Over time, with my clients I was able to share that my clients from the older generations just didn't discuss what they were going through, they just went into their offices and suffered in silence. As I would share this information it began to bridge the gap as they learned that the culture was so different just a few decades ago in the workplace. Thankfully the young generation has pushed so hard for being open that it has begun discussions among people who would have normally stayed silent.

One powerful way to alleviate the loneliness of leadership is by opening up about challenges and seeking support from others. Leaders often face immense pressure to project strength and competence, which can create a sense of isolation. However, by embracing vulnerability and sharing their struggles with trusted individuals, leaders can experience a profound sense of relief and connection. Sharing vulnerabilities allows leaders to express their authentic selves and create space for empathy and understanding. By opening up about challenges, leaders not only lighten their emotional burden but also give others permission to do the same, fostering a culture of openness and support.

Leaders can start by sharing their vulnerabilities with trusted individuals, such as close colleagues, mentors, or friends. These individuals provide a safe and confidential space for leaders to express their concerns, fears, and doubts. Sharing vulnerabilities allows leaders to be seen and understood on a deeper level, strengthening the bonds of trust and creating a support system that can provide valuable guidance and perspective. Through these meaningful connections, leaders can find solace in knowing that they are not alone in their experiences and that others can empathize with their challenges.

There was a time I was mentoring someone at my job and I already knew what I thought was the best way to do something but I decided to ask my guy if he had a recommendation on what to do. This was very intentional for a few reasons. First off, I wanted to see where the guy was at and see how he processes things and comes up with ideas. After all, I wasn't going to be around forever, I wanted to see him come up with a solution where it was safe for me to catch him if he fell. The next thing is I learned a long time ago, that I am not always right and don't always have the most innovative ideas. So although as I said, "I thought" I had the best way, I was also genuinely open to what my mentee had to say in case it was something different, especially if it was something that would be more effective, efficient, cheaper, or just all around better.

Creating a supportive environment begins with fostering open communication and practicing active listening as a leader. When leaders encourage team members to openly express their thoughts, ideas, and concerns, it creates a space where everyone feels valued and heard. By actively listening to what others have to say, leaders show respect and empathy, which in turn encourages further dialogue and collaboration. Open communication helps to break down barriers, encourage diverse perspectives, and build trust within the team. It allows team members to feel comfortable sharing their vulnerabilities and seeking support when needed, ultimately reducing the sense of loneliness in the leadership journey.

To create a truly supportive environment, leaders must also prioritize psychological safety within their teams. Psychological safety refers to an environment where team members feel safe to take interpersonal risks, share ideas, and express themselves without fear of judgment or negative consequences. When leaders establish psychological safety, team members are more likely to open up, share their vulnerabilities, and seek support when facing challenges. This sense of safety creates an atmosphere of trust and collaboration, where individuals feel empowered to contribute their unique perspectives and ideas. By valuing and respecting the opinions of team members, leaders cultivate an environment that nurtures growth, well-being, and mutual support.

Again as I have said, I do believe that some of the young generation is too soft. They need to be a little stronger in general. However, if I could liken psychological safety to something more practical; Back to the gym, we go. If someone decides that they want to get into shape, and maybe learn a few new things, jump rope for example. If they go to a normal gym and meet a bunch of rude people who stare at them and say things like, "Come on, why are you even here, you are pretty weak, you might as well not try lifting any of those heavy weights." And further than that, they notice that the floor has holes and feels very squishy as though it won't hold them. The person is very unlikely to push too hard and lift the most weight they can. They will also likely feel insecure when it comes to pushing or trying something new. I see in my head the person in the movie who is too afraid to try something and so they fake a cramp or say that their base jumping hardware is not secured safely so they can't make the jump. In contrast, if there is an environment that is encouraging and the floor seems solid, the person can step out in confidence and push their limits. They won't feel the need to make up excuses as to why they didn't succeed in trying something.

Leading by example is a powerful strategy for cultivating trust and encouraging open communication within a team. When a leader models vulnerability and authenticity, they create an environment where team members feel safe to do the same. By openly sharing their own challenges, failures, and growth experiences, leaders demonstrate that vulnerability is not a weakness but a strength. This transparency humanizes the leader, making them relatable and approachable. It encourages team members to feel comfortable sharing their own vulnerabilities, perpetuating a sense of trust and connection.

Another fundamental part of demonstrating authentic vulnerability is learning how to apologize and actually do so. If you are adept at taking responsibility and apologizing then that's fantastic. If you aren't yet, you're not alone. There are many people out there who are not good either. My family was notorious for offending each other and then separating for a bit and then when enough time has passed, pretending like nothing happened and moving on. I had to learn to apologize later in life. The hardest thing is when you don't feel like you've done anything wrong but your actions have caused tension in a relationship. Of course, as is with most of the book, what I am saying cannot be applied to every scenario. I also don't want you to take responsibility for another person's poor behavior. But you can and should always take responsibility for what your part is in something.

Additionally, providing opportunities for feedback and input is crucial for building trust and encouraging open communication. Leaders should create a culture that values and welcomes diverse perspectives, actively seeking input from team members. By soliciting feedback and involving team members in decision-making processes, leaders demonstrate respect for their opinions and contributions. This approach empowers team members, making them feel valued and invested in the team's success. When individuals believe their voices are heard and their ideas are considered, they are more likely to engage in open and honest communication, knowing their input is valued.

I encourage leaders to embrace vulnerability and recognize its power in driving positive change. It is through vulnerability that leaders can truly connect with their teams, inspire others, and create an environment of authenticity and trust. By being open, honest, and transparent, leaders create a safe space for their team members to do the same, developing a culture of support and collaboration. Embracing vulnerability requires courage, but it is an essential step toward becoming an impactful and effective leader.

Finally, it is important to emphasize the positive impact that vulnerability can have on both personal and organizational growth. When leaders embrace vulnerability, they create an environment that encourages innovation, creativity, and risk-taking. By celebrating diverse perspectives and providing support systems for personal well-being, leaders enable their teams to thrive and contribute to the overall success of the organization. Embracing vulnerability not only enhances leadership effectiveness but also creates a culture that values empathy, understanding, and continuous improvement.

In conclusion, embracing vulnerability is not a sign of weakness but a testament to a leader's strength and authenticity. By recognizing the benefits of vulnerability, leaders can foster meaningful connections, encourage open communication, and create a supportive environment that enables personal and organizational growth. I encourage all leaders to embrace vulnerability, seek support when needed, and cultivate a leadership style that values and harnesses the power of vulnerability.

For just over a decade now, I have been working with a non-profit organization. They do something that I thought was very weird when I first got around it. They have what they call a culture of affirmation. I first went up to help them with a little consulting and then I just stayed around to help a bit more because I liked the people I met. After a month or so, they asked me to come to their full staff meeting. They introduced me and asked the two people I had been working with most directly to stand up and affirm me. I was so confused and uncomfortable. Hawaii culture and even more so Asian culture doesn't allow for such behavior.

However, I realized it felt like water on the dry desert ground. It was absolutely uncomfortable, but it was an extraordinarily rare occurrence where someone would recognize the effort I had put into something that was simply my job. At the same time, I felt so appreciated and interested in helping more.

Affirmation is not a compliment. A true affirmation is when you acknowledge when someone does something intentionally. For example, "Wow, that lipstick color is pretty." Compliment. Shopping and finding the right color I guess is a little bit of an effort, (not sure myself). However, maybe someone you know has been sharing their journey of changing their eating habits and exercising. You notice that there is a noticeable external change in their appearance, energy, and attitude. Saying, "Wow you look good." That's more of a compliment. An affirmation, in this case, maybe, "James, I can see a big change in you! I see that your physique has changed and you are so much more energetic. I know how much discipline that takes,"

It is very difficult to develop this culture, especially if this is not something you have already been doing as an organization, or in your own life.

Generally, employees come to work because they are looking to pay their bills and not for a pat on their back. However, the quality of their work will dramatically change with that small, "Pat on the back." I am not saying that your team or employees are just messing around and when you tell them they are doing a good job, they will suddenly think, "Okay I guess I'll work hard now."

Not unlike earlier in the book where I talk about how your internal attitude or thoughts will communicate through your body language and your performance, Affirmation can affect people the same way. The person who is working just because it is their job is probably doing the best they can. However, if you encourage them and affirm them, their internal motivation will change because it will cause a strong inherent positivity.

Let me give a more practical example: How does it feel to sit in a 2.5-hour meeting that you don't want to be at vs. sitting in a 2.5-hour action film that you love? One feels never ending and the other seems to end too quickly. How do you work when you are in a great mood vs. How well do you work when you are feeling terrible? By creating a culture of affirmation you are able to develop a place where people are overall more positive without having to do anything completely invasive.

However, creating this culture will start with you. It takes being vulnerable. For me, it is more uncomfortable to receive affirmation than to give. I can't tell you if it was difficult for me to learn to affirm others because it's been so many years that I don't really remember my experience.

It is going to be a strange feeling in the beginning but you can do it. I encourage you to start small. When someone on your team does a good job with something, let them know by simply pointing it out. You can point out growth in someone. When you have a worker who has been very difficult or is very weak in a particular area, when you see even a slight transition, Point it out. Tell that person that you've seen growth in the area. You can also use that opportunity to encourage them to keep on the journey. There is a powerful feeling when you are running a long race and part way through someone is yelling and screaming that you can do it. However, if it is someone you know it is more impactful. If it is someone you care about or looks up to, that impact can be indelible.

Similarly, when someone is affirmed by their leader, they will be deeply affected. As you develop a culture of affirmation those around you will experience that psychological safety we have been talking about. As that happens there will be deeper intimacy among the team thereby limiting the level of isolation you experience as a leader.

AUTHENTICITY: BRIDGING THE GAP

We have discussed vulnerability and its impact in the professional setting, and we have touched a little bit on authenticity but I want to delve a little deeper in this chapter. Authenticity in leadership is crucial. From a practical perspective here are a few things that I believe are directly impacted by being authentic

1. Trust and Credibility: Authentic leaders are genuine and true to themselves, which builds trust and credibility among their followers. When leaders demonstrate authenticity, they show that they are sincere, reliable, and honest in their actions and communications. This nurtures trust and strengthens the relationship between leaders and their teams.

2. Employee Engagement: Authentic leaders create an environment where employees feel safe to express themselves, share their ideas, and contribute to the organization. By being authentic, leaders encourage open communication, active participation, and collaboration. This, in turn, enhances employee engagement and motivation, leading to higher productivity and job satisfaction.

3. Emotional Connection: Authentic leaders connect on an emotional level with their followers. They show empathy,

understanding, and compassion, which helps build strong relationships and evokes a sense of belonging within the team. This emotional connection enables leaders to better understand their employees' needs, concerns, and aspirations, leading to more effective leadership and support.

4. Role Modeling: Authentic leaders serve as role models for their teams. By being true to themselves, they inspire others to be authentic as well. This encourages employees to bring their authentic selves to work, express their ideas and opinions, and contribute to the organization's success. Authentic leaders set a positive example and create a culture that values authenticity and encourages others to embrace their individuality.

5. Adaptability and Learning: Authentic leaders are open to learning and personal growth. They acknowledge their strengths and weaknesses, seek feedback, and embrace opportunities for development. This humility and willingness to learn create an atmosphere of continuous improvement and innovation within the organization.

6. Resilience and Authenticity: Authentic leaders are better equipped to navigate challenges and setbacks. By staying true to their values, they can make difficult decisions, withstand criticism, and maintain their integrity during challenging times. Their authenticity provides a solid foundation and guides them in making decisions that align with their principles and beliefs.

One incredibly important character trait among leaders should be kindness. It must be genuine and not forced. There is a misconception regarding kindness and its relationship to weakness. Nice people are weak and manipulative, kind people's intention is rooted in true compassion for someone. Kindness involves a depth of action that is sincere and doesn't have to feel good for the person receiving it. Niceness is about being agreeable just to be liked or for whatever motivation that person has.

I have been involved in music for many years. I have led many musical teams in church and a few teams outside of my church. There was a young lady who wanted to be on the worship team but was genuinely a bad singer. Now I personally hold the belief that there is a very tiny percentage of people who are incapable of learning to sing. It just takes a greater investment for some than others. This woman was going to take a great deal of investment for herself and for others. If I was nice to her, I would have said, "Great job, you can join the team and sing next week!" However, I am kind, not nice. I ended up recording her and showing her on my computer where she was singing and where she needed to be singing regarding the actual notes, she could now see with her own eyes that she was all over the place as compared to the correct notes. From there I told her that musically she needed to work a bit but I wanted to work with her at that time and I also recommended a few brilliant vocal teachers.

Bear in mind that when it comes to having your singing critiqued vs. perhaps how good you are at something else, even playing an instrument, it is your voice. The sound that comes out of you, it can be a very sensitive process. That said, the one kindness I had to show her was that if she just walked up on stage and began singing, it would have gone badly. I didn't say it to her that bluntly, but I did communicate that she wasn't quite ready. Also, I was very clear that I was willing to invest some of my time to help her prepare. She was a member of my church who was very faithful and had a reputation of good character, I wasn't about to just turn her away without any opportunity for growth.

In the business world, there are many circumstances that will create a similar scenario. Perhaps it won't be quite as intimate as an employee's singing, but it can still be deeply personal when a person takes pride in their work. Finding a way to be kind and deliver news up front and express to your worker that you are not belittling their person or their work, but rather finding a way to communicate that their work didn't meet the standard that you needed. From there expressing that you are for them and for their success you can open the door to a far stronger bonded professional relationship.

When you can develop a culture and reputation for being honest and kind the relationships you have with your cohort and subordinates will flourish dramatically. People will feel comfortable taking risks and stepping out in doing something that could be amazing. Knowing all the while that if something doesn't go well, you will be kind in your response. But if their work goes badly, you won't allow them to make a fool of themselves by just putting it out for others to decide is bad.

If you become known for your integrity and kindness, you will help to break through the barrier that comes from the power dynamic. You can also break down the walls that employees put up in fear of judgment regarding their work.

You have probably heard of Steve Wozniak, he was the creator of the personal computer. He had an idea about creating a personal use computer but while he was working at HP, first off he was very nervous about sharing his idea, but he decided to go for it anyway. HP executives shot him down and has trailed behind Apple ever since. Think about the difference it would have made if the leadership team had been known to be open and supportive. I realize that for every good idea, there are probably thousands of bad ones, Thomas Eddison being the case and point. However in leadership, part of getting things done starts with developing relationships. This works both ways, makes those around you feel able to do their jobs well, and reduces the walls that separate you from them, thereby reducing the loneliness of leadership. My hope for you as a leader is that you will be known as someone who eats, breathes, and lives your product or service and the character that embodies your group's values and mission. When you do, you can develop a very high level of authenticity which will again, open the door for relationships and reduce the isolation you feel as a leader. If you are doing something, then you should definitely believe in it. If you don't, you definitely need to take a moment to look at what you're doing and make some decisions.

In the next chapter, we are going to dive into greater detail about things such as trust and emotional intelligence but I will say here, you can't be authentic if you don't even know what your feelings are. If you don't understand what you are feeling and can't comprehend what those around you are feeling then authenticity is nearly impossible.

Have you ever had someone say to you when you behave a certain way in a heated moment, "You're better than this." Or, "This isn't really you." There are a lot of mixed thoughts regarding this, some people say that those moments are how you can truly know a person. And where that may be partly true, I also believe that a person is who they are based on how they behave. In my experience, the most put-together person with solid character will act out poorly if all the circumstances line up correctly. So in my opinion I don't believe that is "who they are" when someone perhaps has a strong reaction to something in the heat of a discussion. Having someone who can point out that it isn't in keeping with your character is a valuable tool.

As with every other tool from this book, you must be discerning as to who you would be open and honest with. Authenticity is something that you can always have, but how much you share and how open you are will vary based on who you are speaking and interacting with. For the past 10-15 years I have intentionally worked on being true to myself and being honest and kind with everyone around me. I don't always get it right, and honestly, I have found myself apologizing countless times throughout the years. But I have found that my being honest and transparent has opened the door for others every time I have.

Christians talk about the word Testimony. In the Christian

world, that word usually refers to the story of how someone was before they became a Christian, how they became a Christian, and what has happened since. I don't often share my testimony at events these days, however, in my younger days that was quite different. When I would it would be startling the number of times complete strangers would come up to me and say things like, "I didn't know men were allowed to admit they struggle." Or, "I have had similar experiences but I have never told anyone before." I actually developed a client relationship through one such experience. His exact words were, "I have never heard someone be so vulnerable, especially to a group of strangers, can I have your card?" Please recognize I can't take credit for the transformation that took place at that guy's workplace, but I can say that my transparency and authenticity when I spoke, is what my former client credits as his motivation to follow suit. He may have in my opinion dove in a little quick, a little deep, and a tiny bit premature. We laughed as he recounted the entire story and the expression on the face of his inner circle as he went from a locked vault to someone who shared a bunch of feelings with his team. Thankfully, without realizing he had already surrounded himself with people of great character. Although their reactions were jaws nearly hitting the floor and stunned silence for a few minutes. He finally made a joke nervously about tossing M&Ms into their open mouths and everyone started to laugh.

His right-hand man said something to the effect of, "I thought I was the only one who felt that way." At that moment the dam broke. They all began to share about their emotional experiences working at the company, they started talking about things that have really not been working. They shared about how much they valued each other, and how much awe they felt at some of their other coworkers. One person I will call James began to share about how hard the struggle outside of the job was. James opened up about issues with his landlord and how he was basically harassing him because he had told the landlord that the shower faucet was still leaking after 2 months. The landlord would leave notes on his door and send very threatening emails and texts. The landlord was working on ways to kick James out. All the while James didn't have the time or resources to deal with him due to a sibling having been in some sort of accident. James had been using all his spare time to go over and help their family. The room stood still for a moment and then someone said, "I had no idea you were dealing with all of that at home. I am so sorry for blowing up at you the other day." Apparently, the person who just apologized had gotten fed up with James because he was lagging behind on an important deadline. The other employee said, "You gotta speak up if you need help. The deadlines are very important but so is your family. We can pick up some of the slack if we know that you need the help."

James sat there with a slightly sullen look on his face and another employee said, "I have the contact info for one of the housing advocacy groups at my desk I can give to you today." James responded, "No, I can do this on my own. I am not going to be harassed by some landlord." The other employee responded, "No! we know you can do it on your own but you don't have to. We all talk so much about being a team but I don't know if we actually function like one."

This happened in a meeting that was supposed to be about an hour. The meeting ended up taking four! There was so much shared on that day between the team. They shared about things that were happening in their personal lives, some shared about how it made their work more fun, and others more challenging. As my former client shared the next day about the explosion that took place in the office, I was probably more shocked at the outcome than his employees were about his being so open. I asked him how is he feeling now. He said, "I don't know if I have ever been this exhausted and this energized in my life."

Of course, I proselytize the value of vulnerability and authenticity and all of that but the impact it had in this moment is beyond any other experience. I have yet to hear a story where being truthful was a total wash, but again, this story is something else. He ended up contracting me to perform the 5 Behaviors of a Cohesive Team assessment and do an update another 9 months later. The team made strides that I have not seen in another team before. I believe with the openness they expressed in that meeting that I wasn't there for, they were just ready and willing to make the necessary changes.

SOMETIMES YOU NEED TO QUIT

I heard a story of how they catch monkeys in the wild in South East Asia. They will take a barrel and put some bananas in it. They will drill a hole just large enough for a monkey's hand to fit inside. Hunters will lie in wait, a monkey will come up to the barrel and reach inside to grab a banana. When they get a hold of it, their hand can't come back out of the hole while they are holding the banana. However, for some neurological reason, the monkeys will not let go of the banana. The hunter will just walk up to the monkey and grab them. The monkeys will be freaking out but not letting go of the banana so they can run away.

I don't like the word quit. I imagine that you have similar connotations to the word. If I can define the word a little more clinically perhaps we can remove the connotation of "Failure" from the word. A definition of the word "quit" can be: to voluntarily stop or discontinue one's involvement, participation, or pursuit of a particular activity, endeavor, or situation. Quitting involves making a deliberate decision to cease further engagement, often driven by factors such as personal well-being, fulfillment, or a desire for change. It implies a conscious choice to let go, release, or withdraw from something that is no longer serving one's interests, goals, or values. Quitting can be an act of self-reflection, courage, and empowerment, allowing individuals to redirect their energy and resources toward more meaningful or fruitful pursuits.

In this chapter, I am speaking about quitting things that are not adding value to your life or organization. It may mean quitting your job, and it may also mean stopping heading in the direction of doing something that you were excited about, reevaluating, and heading in a different direction. In the journey of leadership, there are times when the path we're on no longer serves us or aligns with our true aspirations. Recognizing these moments and having the courage to quit can be a transformative experience for leaders. We are going to explore the signs and indicators that suggest it may be time for leaders to consider quitting. It is highly important to utilize self-reflection and self-awareness in recognizing when a situation no longer aligns with their values, goals, or vision. Additionally, it delves into the fear and resistance associated with quitting, shedding light on the role they play in delaying the decision.

Identifying the signs that indicate it may be time to quit is crucial for leaders. These signs can manifest in various ways, such as a constant feeling of frustration or stagnation, a misalignment between personal values and organizational culture, or a lack of fulfillment and passion in the work. By exploring these signs and understanding their significance, leaders can gain clarity on when it might be appropriate to consider quitting.

Self-reflection and self-awareness are powerful tools for leaders to gauge their satisfaction and alignment within a given situation. Taking the time to introspect and evaluate whether a current endeavor truly aligns with its values, goals, and vision is essential. It requires leaders to dig deep, listen to their intuition, and honestly assess their level of fulfillment and engagement. Through this process, leaders can gain valuable insights and make informed decisions about whether to continue or quit.

Addressing the fear and resistance associated with quitting is crucial for leaders. The decision to quit often triggers a range of emotions, including fear of the unknown, fear of failure, and fear of judgment from others. Resistance can arise from a sense of loyalty, attachment, or the belief that quitting equates to giving up. By acknowledging and understanding these fears and resistance, leaders can navigate them more effectively and make decisions based on what is truly in their best interest.

In the pursuit of effective decision-making, it is crucial for leaders to engage in a thorough assessment of the costs and benefits associated with their current endeavors. This introspective process entails evaluating the potential consequences of continuing down a particular path. By considering the sacrifices made, such as time, energy, and resources, leaders can gain clarity on whether the investment is still justified.

Exploring the potential risks and drawbacks of persisting in a situation that has lost its value is a vital aspect of this assessment. It requires a candid examination of the negative implications that may arise from clinging onto the familiar, despite its diminishing returns. This introspection enables leaders to recognize potential pitfalls, such as stagnation, missed opportunities, or a decline in overall effectiveness.

Simultaneously, it is essential to contemplate the potential opportunities and advantages that may emerge from letting go and redirecting one's energy and resources toward more promising avenues. Embracing change and releasing attachments can open doors to new possibilities, fresh perspectives, and revitalized growth. Leaders who possess the courage to relinquish the comfort of the familiar in pursuit of greater potential can discover renewed inspiration, enhanced creativity, and increased adaptability.

Ultimately, the process of assessing the costs and benefits of continuing in a particular endeavor empowers leaders to make informed decisions. By honestly weighing the potential risks and drawbacks against the opportunities and advantages, leaders can navigate the complex terrain of leadership with wisdom and clarity, ensuring their efforts align with their vision and contribute to their long-term success.

It's crucial to examine the impact of holding onto something that causes personal stress, burnout, or dissatisfaction. Leaders often find themselves caught in situations that drain their energy, compromise their well-being, and hinder their ability to thrive. By acknowledging and addressing these negative effects, leaders can make more informed choices that prioritize their personal fulfillment and long-term success.

Prolonged involvement in a draining or unfulfilling situation can take a toll on both physical and mental health. The relentless demands, persistent stressors, and lack of personal fulfillment can lead to exhaustion, anxiety, and a decline in overall well-being. It is vital for leaders to recognize the importance of maintaining their physical and mental health as the foundation for effective leadership. Neglecting self-care in favor of persisting in a detrimental situation only perpetuates the cycle of stress and dissatisfaction, ultimately hindering personal and professional growth.

Prioritizing personal well-being must be a central consideration in the decision-making process. Leaders must actively seek out strategies for self-care, setting boundaries, and nurturing their physical, emotional, and mental health. This may involve seeking support from trusted mentors, engaging in regular exercise and mindfulness practices, and cultivating hobbies and interests that bring joy and rejuvenation. By prioritizing personal well-being, leaders enhance their resilience, creativity, and ability to navigate challenges effectively.

In conclusion, examining the impact of holding onto something that causes personal stress, burnout, or dissatisfaction is crucial for leaders. By recognizing the toll on physical and mental health, leaders can make informed decisions that prioritize their well-being. Integrating self-care practices into their leadership journey empowers leaders to thrive personally and professionally, ensuring a sustainable and fulfilling path forward.

I am infamous for not quitting when I feel like I should. It has a lot to do with my stubborn nature. Previously it had to do with the fact that I was trying to prove something. What exactly, I have no idea now, but I needed to prove that I was unrelenting. Ultimately, quitting can open doors to new opportunities, align leaders with their authentic selves, and propel them towards a more fulfilling and purposeful path. A great example is, my first job in construction was working for a roofing company. It was an awful experience one day I nicked a vein in my hand and was bleeding all over the place. I asked if I could go to the hospital to get stitches and their response was, "Is this going to be a workers comp issue?" I should have driven to the hospital and not come back. Sometimes our stubbornness can blind us to the obvious truth. It can be difficult for us to see that the train has gone off the track some time ago. It's our responsibility to decide whether to put the train back on or just leave that train behind.

However, a few months later the company was struggling a lot and they had to lay off two-thirds of the staff. Not surprising based on their treatment of their employees. That to say, my layoff forced me to reach out to some people who connected me with a job during that terrible economic time. When I started working for the new company I was only working ten hours per week at ten dollars per hour. So I was now living under a fifty-two-hour cut each week. But I felt amazing. I was absolutely in love with life as compared to where I was before. My roommates from that time of my life still refer to that time as my zombie season. It truly was. I was waking up at 5 am and getting home at 6:30 exhausted by everything connected to the job. I was not a friendly person in any aspect of my life. I worked Monday through Saturday from 6 am – 6 pm. I was so miserable I couldn't even get to church half the time. When I did, I would leave immediately after lacking any energy to spend time with friends who usually make me feel rejuvenated.

My new company was something different. Yes, I obviously wasn't working as much so that affected my energy level but there was something far more. The atmosphere was so different at the new company. One day, I was called into the VP's office and she says to me, "I understand your motorcycle tires are bald?" I responded awkwardly, "I mean, yeah but they're racing tires, they heat up and stick to the road so no worries." She then asked me, "Why haven't you replaced your tires?" I responded, "They are almost $800 for the pair." She said, "Today after work, I don't care what else you have going on, I want you to go to your motorcycle shop and order new tires. Give them my phone number because I am going to pay for them." I looked at her completely stunned and said, "Why? I don't drive my motorcycle for you, I just drive to work with it and then pick up the truck." Her response is what changed the entire direction of my life, "But you work for us, and so your safety is important to us."

I was mentally broken in that moment. I couldn't wrap my mind around what was happening. I went from a company that didn't care if I bled out or not as long as I wasn't filing for workers' compensation, to a reasonably large investment out of the VP's personal account for my safety outside of work. That was the moment that inspired me to go back to school to figure out the differences between the companies and find what practices could be implemented to replicate this in other businesses.

If I hadn't been let go from my previous company I have no idea what would have happened because I wouldn't have quit on my own. I was stuck in the belief that I couldn't do better, I wouldn't be able to find anything if I did leave. People may not agree with it, but I believe without question that God was the reason I was laid off from that job. I have since gotten a little bit better at leaving something when it truly isn't working out.

I am talking a lot about quitting a job but it doesn't have to be that big of a decision. It could be an initiative that you are working on or an idea that you have been trying to materialize. Sometimes you have to back away from the dream.

If you are needing to quit your job though, you will need to address the potential impact of your decision to leave the organization and its stakeholders. A leader's departure can create a void in the organizational structure, disrupt established workflows, and impact team dynamics. It is important for leaders to anticipate and address these potential challenges proactively. By acknowledging the potential consequences, leaders can take steps to mitigate any negative impact on the organization. This may involve developing a comprehensive transition plan, identifying suitable successors or interim leaders, and ensuring a smooth transfer of responsibilities. By being proactive and transparent about the decision to quit, leaders can help instill confidence in the organization and its stakeholders, fostering a sense of stability during the transition.

Exploring strategies for mitigating the potential negative consequences and managing the transition effect is crucial. Leaders should prioritize open communication and engage in honest conversations with key stakeholders about the decision to quit. By providing clarity and transparency, leaders can alleviate concerns and leave behind a sense of trust and understanding. It is also important to involve relevant team members in the decision-making process and seek their input on potential solutions and alternatives. By including others in the transition planning, leaders can create a sense of ownership and collaboration, minimizing the impact of the departure.

In addition, discussing the importance of open communication, transparency, and succession planning is essential in navigating the aftermath of a leader's departure. Organizations should foster a culture that encourages open dialogue and transparency, allowing for effective knowledge transfer and smoother transitions. Succession planning should be an ongoing process to ensure a pipeline of potential leaders and minimize disruption when a leader decides to quit. By identifying and developing internal talent, organizations can minimize the potential risks associated with leadership transitions and facilitate a seamless handover of responsibilities. Open communication, transparency, and succession planning are key components in preserving organizational stability and continuity in the face of a leader's decision to quit.

By addressing the potential impact, exploring strategies for effective transition management, and emphasizing open communication and succession planning, leaders can navigate the process of quitting with greater confidence and minimize any adverse effects on the organization and its stakeholders. I don't want you to see all of this and retreat from your decision to leave if it is the most healthy decision for you. I want you to be aware that you will leave a hole when you go, but by doing your best to follow the steps above, you can truly transition in the best way possible.

Quitting can actually be an opportunity for growth. Quitting should not be seen as a sign of failure or weakness, but rather as a strategic decision to redirect your energy and resources towards more promising avenues. By reframing quitting in this way, leaders can shift their mindset and embrace the potential for personal and professional growth.

Discussing strategies for reframing quitting as a strategic decision is crucial. Leaders should reflect on their goals, values, and long-term vision to assess whether their current path aligns with their aspirations. By evaluating the potential benefits and opportunities that may arise from quitting, leaders can make informed decisions that pave the way for new possibilities. This may involve exploring alternative career paths, starting a new venture, or pursuing further education and development. Leaders can proactively plan their transition and identify the resources and support they need to make a successful leap into the next phase of their journey.

Exploring examples of leaders who made successful transitions after quitting can provide valuable insights and inspiration. By examining the experiences of those who have navigated similar situations, leaders can learn important lessons about resilience, adaptability, and seizing opportunities. These examples serve as reminders that quitting can lead to new avenues of success and fulfillment. Whether it's entrepreneurs who left stable careers to pursue their passions or executives who made strategic career shifts, there are valuable insights to be gained from these stories. Leaders can draw inspiration from their journeys and apply the lessons learned to their own situations, empowering them to embrace quitting as a catalyst for growth and exploration.

By encouraging leaders to view quitting as an opportunity for growth, discussing strategies for reframing quitting as a strategic decision, and exploring examples of successful transitions, leaders can embrace the notion that quitting can open doors to new possibilities and avenues for success. By adopting this mindset, leaders can make courageous decisions that propel them toward their true potential and create a path of fulfillment and achievement.

The fears associated with quitting can be deeply rooted and can manifest in various ways. One common fear is the fear of feeling embarrassed or judged by others. We live in a society that often celebrates perseverance and resilience, which can make quitting seem like a taboo. The fear of facing criticism or being labeled as a quitter can be a significant barrier that keeps individuals from making the necessary changes in their lives. It takes courage to overcome this fear and prioritize personal well-being over external judgments. However, most people in your life would celebrate you quitting smoking or quitting drinking if you have an issue with too much alcohol. Perhaps making sure that if you feel like you are being judged by someone who is significant in your life, explain to them that quitting is the right choice for your health or the direction of your life. If they are not a significant relationship then they do not merit your time and explanation in response to their judgment.

Another fear that people often grapple with is the fear of leaving things unfinished. We are conditioned to believe that quitting implies failure and that not seeing something through to the end is a sign of weakness. This fear stems from our desire to complete what we start and achieve a sense of accomplishment. However, it is essential to recognize that there are instances when quitting is the wisest decision, and it does not diminish our abilities or achievements. Sometimes, acknowledging that a particular path is no longer serving us or aligning with our values allows us to redirect our energy toward more fulfilling endeavors.

Fear of the unknown is another common obstacle that prevents people from quitting. The familiar can be comforting, even if it no longer brings joy or fulfillment. Stepping into the unknown can be intimidating, as it requires us to venture outside our comfort zones and face uncertainty. It is human nature to seek stability and predictability, but growth often lies beyond the boundaries of familiarity. Overcoming this fear involves embracing the inherent opportunities and possibilities that await us when we are willing to take a leap of faith and quit something that no longer serves us.

Ultimately, it is important to recognize and address these fears surrounding quitting. By acknowledging and understanding these fears, individuals can work towards overcoming them and making decisions that are aligned with their personal well-being and long-term goals. It takes courage to confront these fears head-on and embrace the transformative power of quitting. When we can release the grip of fear and trust in our own judgment, we create space for new beginnings and open ourselves up to a world of possibilities.

LEADING WITH EMPATHY AND EMOTIONAL INTELLIGENCE:

At the end of the previous chapter, I mentioned the 5 Behaviors of a Cohesive Team. If you are leading a team, I want to encourage you to look into it. There is a quite famous book known as The 5 Dysfunctions of a Team. It was the book that initially got me heading in the direction that my life is on now. It is a book that explains there are 5 dysfunctions that a team usually encounters that can cause division or failure to succeed – measuring with whatever metric you have.

The Five dysfunctions are in the form of a pyramid. The base is an absence of trust, When a team doesn't trust each other, there is very little chance of success, and if there is a success, it will be very small since no one will be willing to take risks. The reason I speak about this now after the chapters on Vulnerability and Authenticity is that Lencioni talks about the difference between predictive-trust and vulnerability-based trust. In most professional relationships the "trust" between employees is what he calls predictive-based trust. What that means is that "I know you will react this way because I have seen it happen." Or, "I know that you are going to get the job done on time because you always do."

Vulnerability-based trust is where someone has been open about their strengths and weaknesses so it sounds a little more like, "I know that you can handle the project because you have been open with me about your strengths and weaknesses. If you couldn't handle this you would tell me." Or, "I am comfortable sharing with you that I am having an issue because we have a culture of understanding and allow for each other's shortcomings."

The second dysfunction is Fear of Conflict. This is quite self-explanatory, if you are unwilling to confront an issue for whatever reason, the issue will remain and that can compound into a big problem from the outcome to the ability to maintain the relationships with the team.

Lack of commitment is the third stage of the pyramid. If people aren't committed to seeing the team succeed then it will in fact fail. If a person on the team isn't committed then their workload will fall by the wayside and become a severe problem when the deadline approaches. Also, other teammates will see what that person is doing and the potential for resentment becomes very high.

Number four is the Avoidance of Accountability. If you are avoiding accountability the result of your work may be poor. The team knows that you are not holding up to your end of the deal and again bitterness can grow toward that person. Accountability in general is a vastly powerful and helpful tool.

Finally, the top of the pyramid is Inattention to Results. To me, this has a lot to do with participation trophies. Absolutely, effort is incredibly important but results are as well. How much each thing is important is indexed to the role you are in. I am sure there are a few roles or jobs out there where results aren't as important as effort, but I would say overall results are the final metric for the majority of work.

Years ago, I was coaching a client who was working in sales at a construction company. They were selling a new construction material that would perform better, be more cost-effective, and be environmentally friendly. They were very excited about an upcoming proposal that would be world around 15 million dollars. He worked on the proposal very hard and did a decent job on the presentation. Unfortunately, he didn't quite knock it out of the park. The developer he met with decided to go with the traditional material because he didn't quite sell them on it. In the end, the company had fairly large layoffs because they missed the contract.

His initial response was rather strange to me. I believe it was some sort of defense mechanism. He was sharing with me how great the presentation was and how ready he was and I asked him if he got the contract. He said, he did not, but he created such an amazing presentation. I said back, but, you didn't get the contract. He replied, "Yeah but I did such a great job." And I replied again, "Yes, but you didn't get the contract."

We went back and forth for a bit until it sank in. Please know, that I am not a coach who beats up my clients. This particular client really needed a breakthrough in the understanding that he doesn't get paid if he doesn't make any sales. So he can't survive on effort alone. This is what I mean when I blame participation trophies. Only when you're a child do you win a trophy for not winning or succeeding. Effort is great, with training and grit, effort often becomes success, but effort alone is not enough. Another example is, "Wow, thanks for building me my house. Why doesn't it look anything like the plans and why does it only have 1 bathroom when we had decided that there was supposed to be 4?" Inattention to results.

I bet if you look back at your time in school you will remember group projects where there was one person who did the work, someone who was bossy, someone who showed up on the last day, and whatever role you experienced. The reason is most people know that teams are helpful, but most people don't know how to structure a team. Teachers who put you in groups went to college with the same people you grew up with. They never learned how to appropriately create a team. This is why I highly recommend someone who is certified in the 5 Behaviors of a Cohesive Team.

Having a team that is doing well in cohesion can dramatically impact the sense of loneliness that leaders experience.

As I mentioned before, Emotional Intelligence is very important if you are going to succeed. Emotional intelligence refers to a set of skills and qualities that enable individuals to recognize, understand, and manage their own emotions, as well as perceive and respond effectively to the emotions of others. It encompasses the ability to navigate and harness emotions, both in oneself and in interpersonal relationships. Emotional intelligence involves a combination of self-awareness, self-regulation, empathy, and social skills, all of which contribute to improved communication, decision-making, and overall well-being.

At its core, emotional intelligence involves being attuned to one's own emotions and understanding their impact on thoughts, behaviors, and interactions. This self-awareness allows individuals to accurately recognize and label their emotions, as well as understand their triggers and patterns. By developing this level of self-awareness, you can better manage your emotions and make conscious choices rather than being driven solely by reactive impulses.

Moreover, emotional intelligence includes the ability to regulate and control one's emotions effectively. This involves being able to manage stress, adapt to change, and maintain a balanced emotional state. It also encompasses the capacity to delay gratification, control impulsive reactions, and handle conflicts constructively. By regulating emotions, individuals can make more rational decisions, maintain positive relationships, and cope with challenges in a healthier and more productive manner.

Another critical aspect of emotional intelligence is empathy, which involves understanding and sharing the emotions of others. Empathy allows individuals to connect with and relate to others on a deeper level, demonstrating compassion, active listening, and an ability to consider different perspectives. By practicing empathy, individuals can build stronger relationships, resolve conflicts more effectively, and create a supportive and inclusive environment.

Finally, emotional intelligence encompasses social skills, which are essential for effective communication and building relationships. These skills include verbal and non-verbal communication, teamwork, leadership, and conflict resolution. Individuals with high emotional intelligence can navigate social dynamics, build rapport, and influence others positively.

In short, emotional intelligence is the ability to understand and manage emotions in oneself and others. It involves self-awareness, self-regulation, empathy, and social skills, which collectively contribute to improved personal and professional relationships, effective communication, and overall success in various aspects of life. Developing emotional intelligence is a lifelong journey that can lead to greater self-mastery, emotional well-being, and more fulfilling connections with others.

When you have a high level of emotional intelligence you are able to be aware of your level of energy and how you can feel so drained for what seems like no reason. How you can confront issues within yourself so it doesn't spill over on those you are leading.

Many years ago, I was sitting in a coffee shop where I like to do work at. I was finishing some paper for some degree and a woman walked close to me to get my attention and waved. I waved back and smiled and then looked back at my computer. But she didn't walk past. So I looked back at her and then took my headphones off. She asked me if I would be willing to pray for her. Yes, being transparent, I was busy, had my headphones on, and probably had procrastinated on this paper so I probably needed to get it done quickly. I was not exceptionally excited to stop what I was doing for this person I didn't really know.

I said, "Sure I can pray for you, whatsup?"

She began to share that she has been struggling to be focused at work. She said that she has been working as a skills, but now she really can't focus on what she's doing. I looked at her, and I could sense there were some strong emotions in her statement. It seemed like something more than just a focus issue. I pulled out the chair for her to sit down and I asked her how long she had been struggling. She said around 7 months, I asked her how long she has been doing the same type of work. She said over 20 years. As she sat there I asked her if there was anything that happened around that time. What she said next to me was shocking.

She started to open up about a story where on a major holiday she was off but the child she was working with who was like a son to her wandered off and drowned in a neighbor's pool. She wasn't even working that day but she still felt responsible.

Now a person with no emotional understanding or a low EQ may think, it's been 7 months, it wasn't her child, and she wasn't working so it's not her fault. However, I knew that from the story she shared about the interaction with the parents, she felt that it was because she was better at handling the little boy than the parents so she felt that if she had been around he wouldn't have run away and drowned, thus she was responsible for his death. As we got to talking I knew that it wasn't her fault in any way and she didn't have a burden that she should carry. However, I know that you can't tell someone who is grieving, "Eh, just get over it, it's not your fault." Yet that is the type of thing we do far too often.

In the Christian world, there is this belief that is strange to me. I do believe that God heals people physically, emotionally, and spiritually. But I have heard people imply and even more than imply that if you are spiritual, you should have been healed so either something is wrong or you need to just get over it. The Bible and current science agree, that thinking is inaccurate and generally unhelpful. I shared with the woman that I felt hurt as she shared the story and that I couldn't imagine losing a child, real or Hanai. (Hanai is the Hawaiian word that basically means adopted.)

I told her that she needed to go to her home group and share what she is truly feeling. She can't just go in and say, "Oh yeah, God is good, I feel great." If she is hurting she needs to be honest about it. Hiding the feelings doesn't help them go away. I told her if the group can't handle her saying that every week for the next 3 months or a few years she needs to find another group. I did also tell her that she needs to be praying or talking to someone at the church or a professional counselor if necessary so she can be in motion. But she needs to be honest. At the end of our conversation, she looked me in the eye and said, "Thank you for hearing my pain." I was expecting, and I guess maybe wanting her to say, "Wow, you're smart, a good coach, now I will focus better." But she didn't, the thing she needed was someone to understand that she was hurting.

I checked in with her a few years later (She wasn't a client of mine or a member of my church, she was more of an acquaintance whom I didn't have any regular contact or communication with.) I asked her how she was doing after our conversation. She hadn't come to me to tell me how much she was still hurting, she took it to her small group. She shared with me that it was an extremely difficult year for her. She went through a time that was the hardest she had ever experienced but she was through the storm and doing genuinely well.

There are countless times where a person just needs to be seen and heard and then they can move on. Other times it takes more work and other elements, but sometimes someone says, "Hearing your story I feel _____." This is all it takes for them to say, "Someone knows, and understands. Now I can move on."

As a leader, this took will create bonds between you and your team and your people. When you hear them and communicate to them that you hear them they can be impacted in such a way that they will know they can trust you. The relationship is built from there forward.

WHAT WILL YOUR LEGACY BE?

Maybe 15 years ago I was at a funeral, listening to all the stories shared about the person who had just passed. I was reflecting on my own life and I asked the question that everyone should consider at some point. "If I died today, what would someone say about me at my funeral." I recognize that this will probably only resonate with people who consider themselves Christian, but the only thing that I really want people to say is, "Danny loved like Jesus." At the core of what Christianity teaches is, "Jesus made a sacrifice for the world because the world was disconnected from God." His sacrifice was his life because He loved.

I am not meaning to preach to anyone, this is simply what I realized that I want my legacy to be. Anyone that encountered me in my lifetime would feel cared for and leave feeling respected as a human and hopefully walk away a little better than they were before they met me because I added value to their life. What is the legacy that you want to leave behind?

It is essential to delve into the profound connection between the loneliness of leadership and the significance of shaping a meaningful legacy. I aim to explore the correlation between the loneliness of leadership and the imperative of creating a legacy that withstands the test of time. It is within the depths of this loneliness that leaders have the opportunity to reflect, reassess, and redefine their purpose.

By shaping a leadership legacy, you can embrace the discomfort of breaking free from isolation and stepping into a realm of purpose-driven action. The chapter will illuminate the transformative power that lies within this connection. It emphasizes the notion that leaders must not succumb to the isolation they encounter but rather use it as fuel to ignite their desire to leave a lasting imprint on the world.

Ultimately, I hope to urge you to embrace the connection between your own feelings of isolation and the significance of shaping a legacy that extends far beyond your time in leadership. By understanding and leveraging this connection, leaders can transcend the solitude, leaving behind a legacy that not only echoes their own achievements but also positively impacts the lives of those they lead and the organizations they serve.

A leader's values, purpose, and vision for their leadership legacy serve as the guiding compass that directs their actions and shapes the impact they leave behind. These fundamental elements reflect the core essence of who they are as leaders and what they stand for. In the context of shaping a meaningful legacy, it is crucial for leaders to delve deep into their values, introspectively explore their purpose, and envision the future they aspire to create.

Values, as the bedrock of a leader's character, provide the moral and ethical framework within which they operate. They define the principles that guide decision-making, behavior, and interactions with others. When it comes to shaping a leadership legacy, aligning personal values with organizational values becomes paramount. This alignment ensures that the leader's actions and decisions are consistent with the broader goals and culture of the organization. By doing so, leaders cultivate a sense of unity and coherence, enabling them to make purposeful contributions that resonate with both their personal values and the collective identity of the organization.

At a distilled level, life is just too short. It's too short to be messing around, to be alone or isolated from all the other amazing people that are here on earth. Not to say that you should never schedule time to be alone with your thoughts and for introspection. Rather, to be forced into isolation is highly not worth it. Knowing what your purpose is, your values, and your personal vision will help as a metric to measure your decisions when you are struggling to see what you should do next.

Moreover, a leader's purpose acts as a driving force, fueling their passion and determination to make a lasting impact. It is the deeper "why" behind their leadership journey—the reason that propels them forward even in the face of challenges and adversity. When leaders align their purpose with their leadership legacy, they infuse their actions with intentionality and meaning. By staying true to their purpose, leaders can inspire and motivate others, forging a path toward transformation and progress.

Vision, the ability to imagine a future that is different from the present, plays a crucial role in shaping a leadership legacy. A leader's vision encompasses their aspirations, goals, and the transformative change they seek to bring about. By envisioning a future that aligns with their values and purpose, leaders set a course for action and inspire others to join them on the journey. It is through their visionary mindset that leaders can challenge the status quo, drive innovation, and create a lasting impact that extends far beyond their tenure.

The importance of aligning personal and organizational values in shaping a meaningful legacy cannot be overstated. When leaders embrace this alignment, they create an environment of authenticity, trust, and shared purpose. By ensuring that their personal values align with the values espoused by the organization, leaders create a cohesive and harmonious culture that empowers individuals to contribute their best and work towards a common goal. This alignment also enhances the leader's credibility and fosters a sense of trust and loyalty among their followers.

Mentorship and leadership development play a pivotal role in shaping a leader's legacy. They offer a unique opportunity for leaders to share their wisdom, experiences, and insights with the next generation of aspiring leaders. By nurturing and guiding others, leaders can leave a lasting impact that extends far beyond their own lifetime.

Mentorship is a powerful tool for inspiring and supporting individuals on their leadership journey. It involves creating a nurturing and supportive environment where mentees can learn, grow, and develop their own leadership skills. Through mentorship, leaders can pass on their knowledge, values, and lessons learned, empowering others to reach their full potential.

Leaders who prioritize mentorship understand the importance of investing in the growth and development of their team members. They take the time to identify individuals with potential and provide them with guidance, feedback, and opportunities for growth. By serving as role models and mentors, leaders can inspire others to embrace their own leadership abilities and contribute to the collective success of the organization.

Leadership development programs are also instrumental in shaping a leader's legacy. These programs focus on equipping individuals with the necessary skills, knowledge, and competencies to excel in their roles. They provide opportunities for leaders to enhance their self-awareness, emotional intelligence, communication, and decision-making abilities.

By investing in leadership development, leaders create a culture of continuous learning and growth within their organization. They perpetuate an environment where individuals are encouraged to challenge themselves, embrace new opportunities, and expand their leadership potential. Through leadership development programs, leaders can develop a pipeline of capable and empowered leaders who can carry on their legacy.

DEVELOPING RESILIENCE

Developing resilience is one of the key traits of a leader. The hard truth is, no matter how well you build your team, no matter how much intimacy you create, you will in fact have moments of being alone. How you are in those times, how hard they are, and how you come out of it will depend on your resilience. A pastor of mine was given a prophetic word from someone; In the context of Christianity, a prophetic word refers to a message or revelation believed to be directly communicated by God through a prophet or someone with the gift of prophecy. It is considered a divine utterance that reveals God's will, purpose, or future events. A prophetic word can provide guidance, correction, encouragement, or a warning to individuals, communities, or even nations. It is believed to be inspired by the Holy Spirit and carries authority and spiritual significance. Prophetic words are often seen as a means through which God communicates His love, truth, and direction to His people, inviting them to align their lives with His divine plans and purposes.

The word was, "You need to develop crocodile skin!"
If I remember the story correctly, he was a younger leader who was beginning to walk in a leadership role that was a slightly more pioneering direction. There was an event where he was speaking

at a conference and some influential leader told their group not to attend the pastor's talk. The pastor was very hurt because, well he is a very kind man and genuinely wants the best for those around him. It was after that the word of having crocodile skin was spoken to him.

Even God knows that in the realm of being a leader, you are going to make people mad, you may hurt someone. No matter how stellar of a leader you are, there is no way to make everyone happy. I will say that you should do your best to make decisions that are best for everyone, or as many people as possible, but don't be consumed by the people who get the short straw or have an issue with you just because. You too need crocodile skin, or at least very strong resilience.

Resilience, in the context of the character of a human, refers to the ability to adapt, bounce back, and maintain psychological strength and well-being in the face of adversity, challenges, or significant life changes. It is the capacity to withstand and recover from difficult circumstances, setbacks, or traumatic events, while still maintaining a sense of purpose, optimism, and overall psychological health.

Resilience involves the ability to effectively cope with stress, adversity, or trauma by utilizing personal resources, skills, and support systems. It is not about avoiding or denying difficult experiences, but rather about developing the inner strength and skills necessary to navigate and overcome them. Resilient individuals are able to maintain a positive outlook, regulate their emotions, and effectively problem-solve in the midst of challenging situations.

Furthermore, resilience is not a fixed trait but can be cultivated and developed over time through various strategies, such as building social connections, seeking support, practicing self-care, developing problem-solving skills, fostering optimism, and cultivating a growth mindset. It involves learning from failures, adapting to change, and developing a sense of purpose and meaning in life.

Interestingly people who have experienced a lot of trauma often have a high level of resilience. Now, it doesn't mean because you have experienced great trauma, you are great and that's all, I do recommend dealing with that trauma and its effects but it can be one of the silver linings of what you have experienced.

I knew a very strong leader who had the most interesting trait about him. He could have the most incredibly difficult day at work, do whatever he could to fix the problem then go to bed. The next day it was as if the emotions of the previous day never existed. The problem may still be there but he would be completely new with a brand new level of energy to tackle it. One season he was sharing something about a tech problem he was having. Whereas my understanding of IT and developing computer programs is quite limited, the concept was very clear. He had a project that was needing to come to a close and one of the programmers was very ill. The programmer was supposed to deliver his portion around a week prior to this particular night we were talking. He said that the programmer is brilliant, which is great when he is there, but horrible when he isn't because no one else can pick up where he leaves off. So this put the project at a standstill. My friend was stuck and couldn't get things to move forward and was running high emotionally and low on energy as the day came to a close, he was only closer to the deadline and not the resolution of the project.

As he shared, I could tell he was just drained and done. I imagined that the project would just fall apart and he would have to experience severe consequences. However, the next day we met up for lunch and he was a different man. Still in the same predicament but ready again to take on the challenge. That's the type of resilience we need.

Some more practical ways to develop resilience are:

1. Cultivate a growth mindset: Embrace the belief that challenges and setbacks are opportunities for growth and learning. View failures as stepping stones toward success and focus on the lessons learned from each experience.

2. Build a strong support network: Surround yourself with positive and supportive individuals who can provide guidance, encouragement, and perspective during challenging times. Seek out mentors, coaches, or trusted colleagues who can offer guidance and support.

3. Practice self-care: Prioritize self-care activities that promote physical, mental, and emotional well-being. Engage in regular exercise, practice mindfulness or meditation, get enough sleep, and maintain a healthy work-life balance. Taking care of yourself enables you to better handle stress and challenges.

4. Develop problem-solving skills: Enhance your ability to analyze problems, identify potential solutions, and make informed decisions. Learn to break down complex challenges into manageable steps and seek creative solutions to overcome obstacles.

5. Increase your emotional intelligence: Cultivate self-awareness, empathy, and effective communication skills. Understand your own emotions and reactions, as well as those of others, and learn how to manage them in a constructive manner. Effective emotional intelligence allows for better resilience in dealing with conflicts and challenges.

6. Embrace flexibility and adaptability: Recognize that change is inevitable and develop the ability to adapt to new circumstances. Embrace a flexible mindset that allows for adjusting plans and strategies as needed. This adaptability enables you to navigate uncertainties and bounce back from unexpected situations.

7. Seek continuous learning and growth: Foster a mindset of continuous learning and seek opportunities to expand your knowledge and skills. Stay curious, seek feedback, and actively pursue personal and professional development. Embracing learning allows for greater adaptability and resilience in the face of new challenges.

Resilience is a skill that can be developed and strengthened over time. By practicing these strategies consistently, you can enhance your ability to bounce back from adversity and thrive in the face of challenges. Also, remember that it probably won't happen immediately. It will be a struggle and there will be times when things don't seem like they will finish well. But you need to trust in the process of your growth and just decide that no matter what you won't give up.

Most of the above we have gone into in other chapters but those we haven't I want to expound upon a little. A growth mindset is a belief system that embraces the idea that our abilities and intelligence can be developed through dedication, effort, and learning. It's the belief that we can improve and grow, rather than being limited by our inherent traits or current skill set. People with a growth mindset see challenges as opportunities for growth and view failure as a stepping stone toward success.

When individuals have a growth mindset, they are more likely to embrace challenges, persevere in the face of setbacks, and put in the necessary effort to achieve their goals. They understand that abilities can be developed through hard work, practice, and seeking new strategies. This mindset allows them to approach tasks and problems with a sense of optimism and determination.

In practical terms, developing a growth mindset involves shifting our perspective and internal dialogue. Instead of thinking, "I'm just not good at this," or "I'll never be able to do it," individuals with a growth mindset say, "I may not be good at it yet, but with practice and effort, I can improve," or "I can learn how to do it if

I put in the time and dedication."

To cultivate a growth mindset, it is important to recognize and challenge fixed mindset thinking patterns. This includes reframing failures as opportunities for learning, focusing on effort and the process rather than just the outcome, seeking feedback and constructive criticism as valuable insights for growth, and embracing challenges as chances to expand skills and knowledge. By cultivating a growth mindset, individuals can unlock their full potential, overcome obstacles, and achieve higher levels of resilience in the face of adversity. This is different from a lack of attention to results. It is rather, once the results have happened, turn the event where the target wasn't reached into a learning experience.

We have gone over building a support network a great deal already but since I cannot overstate the value of having one I will provide one last example. I was born and raised in Hawaii, so Coconut trees are very common on the shoreline of the island. There is something that is so fascinating about the way Coconut trees grow. They have adapted to the challenge of the ever-shifting sands and the shallow depth before the very hard lava rock beneath. Coconut tree roots spread out very wide rather than deep. But more than that, they actually intertwine their roots with surrounding Coconut trees. This allows them to develop a vast network that means no matter how hard the wind blows, they just bend with it and then stand back up. Also, the system helps keep the sand from being washed away by the constant waves.

We as people can create our life-teams and professional networks so we can weather the storms that come in our work. If we can learn to depend on each other we are not only able to keep from being broken down ourselves, but we can also support those around us and keep the company from being washed away.

Developing problem-solving skills is an essential aspect of effective leadership. Leaders are often confronted with complex challenges that require innovative solutions. In order to cultivate strong problem-solving abilities, leaders must adopt a proactive and strategic approach.

First and foremost, problem-solving skills require a mindset that embraces challenges as opportunities for growth. Leaders must cultivate a curiosity-driven attitude that fuels their desire to explore different perspectives and uncover underlying causes. This mindset encourages them to approach problems with an open and creative mindset, seeking out unconventional solutions.

Additionally, to continue developing problem-solving skills, leaders should prioritize continuous learning. They can engage in self-study, attend workshops, or seek out mentors who can provide guidance and share valuable insights. By expanding their knowledge and expertise, leaders enhance their ability to analyze complex situations, identify patterns, and generate innovative ideas.

Collaboration is another key aspect of problem-solving. Leaders should actively engage their teams in the process, valuing diverse perspectives and encouraging active participation. By fostering a collaborative environment, leaders tap into the collective intelligence and creativity of their team members, enabling them to tackle complex problems from different angles.

In addition, effective problem-solving involves breaking down complex challenges into smaller, manageable tasks. This allows leaders to focus on specific aspects of the problem, analyze data, and gather relevant information. They can then develop action plans, set clear goals, and assign responsibilities to team members, ensuring that everyone understands their role in finding a solution.

Leaders should embrace a systematic approach to problem-solving. This involves defining the problem, gathering data, analyzing the information, generating potential solutions, evaluating alternatives, and implementing the chosen course of action. By following a structured problem-solving process, leaders enhance their ability to make informed decisions and achieve desired outcomes.

Flexibility and adaptability are crucial qualities for leaders in today's constantly changing world. As I mentioned earlier, the ability to embrace and navigate uncertainties is vital for success. In the face of ever-evolving circumstances, leaders must be willing to adjust their plans, strategies, and approaches. They understand that rigidity and resistance to change can lead to missed opportunities and hinder growth. To be clear, I am from an island, if you have ever seen the Disney movie Moana, the illustration of the people where "Everything is already okay, we don't need to change anything." Is strong! And it is genuinely strong within me as well. So I am not suggesting you learn to be flexible without knowing how difficult that can be for some.

Embracing flexibility means being open to new ideas, perspectives, and possibilities. It involves challenging traditional norms and being willing to explore innovative solutions. A flexible leader recognizes that what worked in the past may not be effective in the present or future, and they are willing to let go of outdated practices or strategies. A leader who embraces adaptability understands that change is inevitable and can be a catalyst for growth. They proactively seek opportunities to learn, evolve, and acquire new skills that will enable them to navigate challenges and seize emerging opportunities.

In practical terms, embracing flexibility and adaptability requires cultivating a growth mindset. It involves fostering a culture of continuous learning and encouraging team members to embrace change as an opportunity for personal and professional development. A leader who embodies these qualities sets an example for their team, inspiring them to be agile, resilient, and open to change.

Moreover, embracing flexibility and adaptability requires effective communication and collaboration. Leaders must engage with their team, actively listen to their insights and ideas, and create an environment where diverse perspectives are valued. This collaborative approach allows for a collective exploration of possibilities and promotes a sense of ownership and commitment to the team's goals. By embracing rather than resisting the potential discomfort of adapting to change, leaders position themselves and their teams for success in an ever-changing landscape. They demonstrate resilience, creativity, and a willingness to challenge the status quo. Through their example and guidance, they inspire their team members to embrace change, learn from setbacks, and continuously adapt to achieve both individual and collective success.

Something I learned on the journey to becoming a coach is to just stay curious. This should be a natural byproduct of being a continuous learner. The practice of staying curious can have powerful implications for a leader. You will end up with people enjoying opening up to you because you are genuinely interested in what they have to say, thus creating greater intimacy and deepening the professional relationship.

On January 15, 2009, a man named Captain Sully, a remarkable pilot, emerged as a hero for his extraordinary act of bravery and skill that saved the lives of all passengers on US Airways Flight 1549. With a calm and composed demeanor, Captain Sully demonstrated exceptional leadership and decision-making under immense pressure. His quick thinking and expertise were on full display when the plane encountered a critical bird strike shortly after takeoff, resulting in the loss of both engines.

In the face of this dire situation, Captain Sully made a split-second judgment to land the aircraft on the Hudson River. With precise maneuvering and exceptional control, he successfully executed a water landing, ensuring the safety of everyone on board. His exceptional piloting skills, honed over decades of experience, were instrumental in averting a catastrophe.

Captain Sully's actions not only showcased his remarkable piloting abilities but also highlighted his unwavering commitment to the safety and well-being of his passengers. His calm and collected leadership in the face of adversity provided a sense of reassurance to everyone on board, and his decisive actions undoubtedly saved countless lives.

Captain Sully's remarkable feat earned him widespread recognition and admiration, turning him into an iconic symbol of heroism and resilience. His story serves as a testament to the importance of exceptional training, experience, and leadership in times of crisis. Captain Sully's selfless and courageous act will forever be remembered as an inspiring example of the power of human resilience and the ability to triumph in the face of extraordinary challenges.

Anyone who has developed a level of mastery in a particular area will also inherently develop what Dr. Patrick Carnes, calls an expert system. This is a system of thinking and understanding that happens automatically as a result of thousands of hours of doing the same thing over and over. For example, I was a stage performer from the time I was around 4 years old. That is also the same time that I started annoying the sound tech, asking question after question. By the time I was 16, a friend and I began our own sound company doing sound for concerts, weddings, and school dances. I have designed around 30 sound systems for churches and high-end homes. I have logged about 12,000 hours sitting behind the soundboard for church bands, big concerts, and events.

When I started working in the church world with sound volunteers who were just really excited to help but had no experience, I would see things fail and the expression was one of complete confusion. I didn't realize the comparison of how much experience because I never really compiled the years of experience in my mind. However when I am sitting at the board and there is a major problem I will know exactly what happened or be able to figure it out within moments, then fix the problem. Whereas while I am training people, or when there is a newer person running things on their own, I will often have to go over to help.

There was a time when one of the new guys was struggling to deal with some issues that had popped up. I was there and was able to help him get back on track. However, he was a little shaken up by the problem and not being able to fix it quickly. His time to recover mentally and emotionally was directly indexed to the amount of time it took him to fix the initial problem. Running a soundboard is clearly different than flying a plane where there are lives at stake. That said if you are at an event with 5,000 people and there are sound issues; there is little comparison to the chill that goes down your spine from all 5,000 people turning to look at you with contempt. No one looks at or thanks a sound person when they do their job. They do however let you know when you haven't done it well.

Coaching is also an area in which I have begun to develop an expert system in as well. I have had multiple scenarios where someone tapped into something that was the true root of the issue and in the early days, I would have definitely missed it. However, I have learned to recognize the signs of someone on the crux of discovery. Now I am able to pivot and go in a completely different direction without even thinking when the opportunity to chase an important rabbit.

In your work, you have probably developed or are developing an expert system and you don't even realize it. There are split-second decisions that you make and don't realize that no one else would have done the same thing in your shoes.

This could be more related to how they have trained bank tellers on how to spot counterfeit bills. There was a story of a group of bank tellers that were sent to a week-long training. During the training, they only handled authentic US currency. It may seem strange that at counterfeit training they were never given counterfeit currency to identify right? The tellers became so comfortable with handling real money that the moment something touched their fingers that wasn't real they knew instantly. They knew what the texture, weight, smell, color, and size should be, so if it didn't match what they were accustomed to, then they would know it was fake. As you have developed mastery in your respective field, you will be able to tell as well that something is off, and with your earned skills, be able to fix things and get them back on track quickly.

These skills that you have developed are what allow for resilience where others may not have any. If resilience is the ability to bend and not break then your knowledge of what to do and your ability to move with changes and challenges is how to prevent breaking down.

FINAL THOUGHTS

As I have written this book and thought of the stories leaders have shared, and how they describe how alone they have felt being isolated, it has really fired my heart up to see leaders find true connections. I believe that leadership is a very noble goal, it is one that can leave an indelible mark on the world and people's lives. It comes with great sacrifice, but I think that with some of the tools we have discussed here, the sacrifice may be a little smaller.

As we reflect on the key themes and insights from the preceding chapters, one overarching message becomes clear: leadership is a journey of self-discovery, growth, and impact. Throughout this book, we have delved into the various aspects of leadership, exploring the challenges, complexities, and rewards that come with leading others.

A fundamental takeaway is the significance of self-reflection in leadership. It is through introspection that we gain deeper insights into our values, purpose, and vision as leaders. By taking the time to understand ourselves, our strengths, and areas for improvement, we can cultivate a greater sense of authenticity and align our actions with our core values.

Continuous growth is another pivotal element of effective

leadership. The willingness to challenge ourselves, step outside our comfort zones, and embrace discomfort is what propels us forward on our leadership journey. It is a commitment to personal and professional development, seeking new experiences, and acquiring new knowledge and skills that enable us to adapt and thrive in an ever-changing landscape.

Throughout this book, we have explored the loneliness of leadership, the weight of responsibility, and the challenges of leading toxic individuals. We have examined the power of vision, the importance of empathy and emotional intelligence, and the value of setting boundaries. We have learned that leadership is not a solitary endeavor, but one that requires collaboration, mentorship, and a genuine connection with others.

As leaders, it is our responsibility to leave a lasting impact, to shape a meaningful legacy. This requires us to lead with purpose, integrity, and a deep sense of empathy. It calls for us to create environments that foster growth, empower others, and inspire greatness. By embracing the discomfort of breaking isolation, we can forge connections, build bridges, and make a positive difference in the lives of those we lead.

I believe I have said it a few times, but I want to remind you that the role of a leader just comes with an element of loneliness that cannot be avoided. This is part of the job responsibility that must be understood before you take the job. But this loneliness can be productive if you allow it to be. In times when it cannot be avoided, we are presented with a unique opportunity for personal growth and transformation. It is during these moments of introspection and quiet reflection that we can delve deep into our inner selves, exploring our thoughts, emotions, and aspirations with a heightened sense of clarity. Solitude offers a sanctuary for self-discovery, allowing us to unravel layers of our being, confront our fears and limitations, and cultivate a deeper understanding of who we are and what truly matters to us. It is within the stillness of solitude that we can embark on a journey of self-transformation, shedding old beliefs and patterns that no longer serve us, and embracing new perspectives and possibilities. As we embrace solitude, we open ourselves to the power of self-reflection, self-awareness, and self-care, paving the way for personal growth, resilience, and a profound connection with our true selves.

While discussing the writing of this book, someone told me that the growth they have experienced in the past three years while they were struggling with feeling alone couldn't have been done if they were in a group. It was in their isolation that they were able to grow into who they were meant to be as a leader.

Being self-aware is paramount for your success as a leader and for building connection with those around you. Understanding your strengths and weaknesses can aid in being free from potential self-consciousness that can damage true intimacy with those around you and further isolation. But that takes being open to vulnerability. I want you to know that, although I am just writing a book, I believe in you and your ability to build and learn to build connection and relationship with people.

My only hope for you in writing this book is that you find your life-team, and develop connections with people around you. Through that, the loneliness that you have been feeling that caused you to pick up this book would be broken and kicked out of your life. It is likely to be an uncomfortable journey, but it is worth it. It's worth it because you shouldn't have to lead alone, but also, there are people missing out on the true you that you have held close and even hidden. Now it's time for action, go and take the risks and see what happens!

Sources:
Fursenko, A., & Naftali, T. (2006). "One Hell of a Gamble: Khrushchev, Castro, and Kennedy, 1958-1964." WW Norton & Company.

Allison, G. T., & Zelikow, P. (1999). "Essence of Decision: Explaining the Cuban Missile Crisis." Longman.

McPherson, J. M. (1988). Battle cry of freedom: The Civil War era. Oxford University Press.

New International Version. (1984). Proverbs 30:21-22.

D'Antonio, M. (2006). Hershey: Milton S. Hershey's Extraordinary Life of Wealth, Empire, and Utopian Dreams. Simon & Schuster.
Hershey Community Archives: The Hershey Story.

Schultz, H., & Yang, D. (2012). Pour Your Heart Into It: How Starbucks Built a Company One Cup at a Time. Hachette Books.

Michelli, J. A. (2018). The Starbucks Experience: 5 Principles for Turning Ordinary into Extraordinary. McGraw-Hill Education.

Clark, T. (2011). The Starbucks Story: How the brand changed the world. Crimson Publishing.

Lencioni, P. (2002). The five dysfunctions of a team: A leadership fable. Jossey-Bass.

Carnes, P. (2009). Recovery Zone, Volume 1: Making Changes that Last: The Internal Tasks. Gentle Path Press.

ABOUT THE AUTHOR

Danny Jones is an accomplished author, consultant, and executive coach specializing in leadership development and organizational effectiveness. With a deep passion for empowering leaders and guiding them toward their fullest potential, Danny has dedicated his career to helping individuals and organizations navigate the complexities of leadership.

Danny holds a Master's degree in Executive Coaching and Consulting from the esteemed Townsend Institute at Concordia in Irvine. This rigorous program equipped Danny with a comprehensive understanding of leadership dynamics, organizational psychology, and effective coaching techniques. He also holds a Master's in Organizational Leadership.

With the publication of 'Loneliness of Leadership,' his third book, Danny explores the profound challenges and unique experiences faced by leaders in today's fast-paced and interconnected world. Drawing on his extensive expertise and research, Danny delves into the depths of leadership loneliness and offers invaluable insights, strategies, and practical solutions to support leaders in overcoming isolation and cultivating impactful leadership.

As an engaging speaker and trusted advisor, Danny has delivered keynote presentations, facilitated workshops, and provided coaching to a diverse range of clients, including churches, non-profit organizations, and businesses. His holistic approach, rooted in empathy, authenticity, and a deep understanding of human behavior, has earned Danny a reputation as a respected thought leader in the field.

Driven by his unwavering commitment to fostering personal growth and transformation, Danny continues to inspire and empower leaders worldwide. Through his books, coaching engagements, and wide range of trainings, Danny is dedicated to helping leaders thrive, forge meaningful connections, and create lasting impact in their organizations and beyond.

For consultation, visit us at www.IHIcoaching.com

www.ingramcontent.com/pod-product-compliance
Lightning Source LLC
Chambersburg PA
CBHW051616120626
46551CB00014B/1816